The **Arky**
TRILOGY

The **Arky**
TRILOGY

Plays by

David Epstein

Retriever Press
AN IMPRINT OF RIVERTOWNS BOOKS

Paperback edition ISBN-13: 978-1-953943-35-4
Electronic edition ISBN-13: 978-1-953943-36-1

LCCN Imprint Name: Retriever Press
Library of Congress Control Number: 2023941286

Retriever Press is an imprint of Rivertowns Books. Copies of this book are available from all bookstores, other stores that carry books, and online retailers. Requests for information and other correspondence may be addressed to:

Retriever Press
240 Locust Lane
Irvington NY 10533
Info@rivertownsbooks.com

To Kate, through every hurricane, drought, tsunami, and dreaded frozen mix, with abiding love.

Contents

Preface

THESE THREE PLAYS were written over a period of five years. By the time I finished *Arky,* my playwriting tank was on empty. I had been writing plays for better than four decades, but the trilogy took me to a place I didn't know I had been hunting. Or was that place hunting me? I found out when I got there.

Ordinarily I would have sent the plays out to producers and regional theatres, but I never did. I have resisted for many reasons, some of which are easier to explain than others. For now, I've decided to put the trilogy between book covers.

Plays are written for the light of the stage. They exist on the page, they come to life in production. If written, directed, performed, and produced well, they will take flight. And if at their core they illuminate something essential about the human spirit, the lights of the stage may become magical lights and thrilling nights may happen.

We all live for those experiences, breathe and sweat for them. We do our best to put our plays up and take our chances. I believe in these three plays. I believe they will find their light. Until then, here they are.

David Epstein
July, 2023

MAHALO

A Play in Three Acts

ACT ONE

In the dark: the sound of breaking glass.

LIGHTS bump up on ARKY, 21, muscular, bare-chested. In a feral rage, he steps towards his father, MICAH, 50s.

ARKY

You don't tell me what to do!

MICAH
(shocked, holds his ground)
All I asked you to do was put a shirt on in the—

ARKY
(thumps his chest)
You—don't—tell—me—what—to—do!
          (closer, flexes his biceps, raises his fists)
I can do whatever I want!

MICAH
(firmly)
Not in this house.

Arky gets right in his face. Micah stares at him, hands at his side, in fists. This could explode.

ARKY

Whatever I want!

He thumps his chest again, snarling. Micah doesn't move.

WOMAN'S VOICE (O.S.)

Micah? What's going on?

Arky backs off as Tess, 50, enters half-dressed.

MICAH

(his eyes never leave Arky)

Stop. Watch your feet.

TESS

(looks down)

What—what happened? Arky?

MICAH

Arky threw a beer bottle through the window because I asked him to wear his shirt.

TESS

(stunned)

He—you what? Arky??

MICAH

(to Arky)

And he's going to calm down now. He's going to calm down.

A beat. Tess steps carefully towards Arky, who is huffing furiously.

TESS

(starts to reach out)

Arky.

ARKY
(low, menacing)

Don't touch me.

TESS
(retracts her hand, fast)

Okay. Please. Go outside now.

Arky looks back at Micah, then slowly, arms raised in fists,
turns and exits.

TESS

Micah—for god's sake.

MICAH

I just asked him to put his shirt on in the house.

TESS

Drunk? Is he drunk? Is he stoned?

MICAH

I don't know what he is anymore.

TESS
(hesitates)

I'll go talk to him.

MICAH
(watching for Arky)

Don't go near him.

TESS

He's upset.

MICAH

He's not reasonable, Tess.
(turns to her)
He's dangerous.

She looks up, surprised by the word.

LIGHTS DROP. In the dark, we hear airport sounds and voices.

LIGHTS RISE on a stage of ramps and platforms. On one platform is a palm tree. On another is a kitchen table and three chairs. On a third is a single, white-sheeted bed. At least one platform is empty.

MICAH and TESS cross together from stage left to right, rolling luggage.

Five steps behind them comes extra-tall ARKY, wearing six-inch high kotherni—platforms strapped to his feet. He moves deliberately—a crane carrying a duffle bag. They stop, wait. He arrives looming over them, and they are about to move again when Micah turns, steps downstage, speaks to the audience.

MICAH

Aloha.

(a beat)

We are going there.

(points to a palm tree)

And we are coming from there, and there.

(points to kitchen and bedroom)

This trip—I want to turn this trip, this entire— "experience" into —an entertainment. It might not work. No, that's the wrong approach. This will be extraordinarily engaging! Watch.

(cues music, executes a neatly turned soft-shoe)

We'll do more of that. The trip goes forward, west, and the story goes back and forth in time. I'll fill you in as we move along. A few songs, too. For fun.

TESS

(ironic)

For fun.

MICAH

Tess doesn't agree with me about—this—this dialogue. That I shouldn't be exposing us. I need to do it.

AIRLINE VOICE

"We are pre-boarding families with small children and any passengers with disabilities."

Very slowly, Micah turns and glances up at his son, who looks down at him.

They share a half-smile before moving off-right.

MICAH
(stops, turns back to the audience)
Sometimes you gamble because you're desperate. You make a decision, a sharp left. You don't know where it will take you, but you
hope for the best and you . . .

TESS
Micah, come on.

MICAH
. . . get on board. A different landscape, another ocean. Mahalo.

*Rolling their luggage, they move off-right. Arky hesitates.
He stares at the audience a moment, then plods after his
parents, and off.*

LIGHTS SHIFT

*Stepping into a spotlight is Beezie, their twenty-five- year-
old daughter. She has a microphone in hand as she addresses her stand-up audience.*

BEEZIE
(with mike, laughs)
Okay, so listen. You can't be too careful about your parents. Believe me, you've got to watch them every second. I mean—there
are two of them. And they can be very clever—like raptors.
(confidentially)
They actually believe that whatever they do they are acting in
your best interests. Please. They're just people—most of them.

(a beat)

So take my little brother, their dream son-scholar-athlete-mes-
siah—now a totally off-the-wall stoner, okay? We're talking
about an Extra-Large, who gets loaded or high and transforms
into this rabid, drooling Doberman.

(shakes her head)

But he's just a big gorgeous baby. A sweetheart. Everybody loves
him. Everybody. Except now I come home for a weekend—and
he won't agree to anything: to work, where to live, what to drink,
when to stop, refuses suggestions, gets nasty, belligerent. And
they don't know what to do. They're totally stumped. Have you
ever seen your parents stumped? It's— "unsettling," okay? He's
breaking the silent contract, you know? We will wipe the butt,
mop the puke, feed, clothe, educate and love, all you have to do is
fake-smile, semi-cooperate, and occasionally whisper: love you,
too. But he won't. Won't listen—refuses—to anyone. Yells, snarls
—they're living with an in-house terrorist. He's really scaring
them.

(a beat)

What exactly is happening here? Is this my family? This can't be
my family. My family is supposed to be a regular, totally normal
family.

(grins)

Like yours.

Arky stands with his duffle bag.

*Separately, from different playing areas, Tess and AVA,
their older daughter, confront Micah who has just walked
into the house.*

AVA

There is nothing wrong with him.

MICAH

Well, he's—let me get my coat off.

AVA

He's just doing too many drugs, Dad.

MICAH

We know that.

AVA

And drinking. That's all it is.

TESS

I'm—I realize I'm frightened to be left alone with him.

MICAH

What?

AVA

It's these kids, these friends. This guy Brent? He's obscenely rich.

MICAH

What are you talking about, Tess?

TESS

Last night when you were in the city. I'm—uneasy.

AVA

He hands out drugs like Fritos.

MICAH

Did he do anything? He's never.

TESS

I moved my bureau against the bedroom door. He was yelling—awful things at me.

AVA

He doesn't need money. He gets stuff.

MICAH

You—your bureau?

AVA

You've got to get him away from these asinine boys. He'll be fine.

TESS

I—it was a precaution.

MICAH

We can't stop him from seeing his friends, Ava.

TESS

I didn't want to upset you on the phone. I didn't sleep all night.

MICAH

Well.

(a beat)

He won't see a therapist. And until he acknowledges he has a problem he can't enter a rehab. They won't take him.

(looks from one to the other)

What do you suggest?

AVA

I don't know! I've got enough stress. He's not my responsibility.

TESS

Maybe a lock. The bedroom door. For when you're away. A lock.

Micah, rattled, takes it all in, then the three travelers move along.

Tess steps downstage into a warm light.

TESS

(sings)

I was living the quotidian life
Occasional pleasures, the usual strife
Kids' angst, kids' romances
Their demands, our finances
When out of the blue it all ripped and it tore
Suddenly I'm bitch, I'm suddenly called whore

What do you do when life pulls out the rug under you
Tell me what do you do?

Lie awake every night
Cataloging your errors

Freezing and sweating through
Endless night terrors?
French roast at six
(not exactly a fix)
A shower at dawn
Food in, shoes on
Hair brushed, big yawn
Just keep keeping on?

Is that what do you do
When life pulls the rug out under you?

On line, on the phone
I'm dumbstruck and numb
But I stumble along
Cause I'm needed I'm strong
Singing this goddam song
Wondering what in the world I can do?

A police siren. We see flashing patrol car lights.

*Tess and Micah, disheveled, agitated, are on the kitchen
platform. Arky has not moved with his duffel bag.*

TESS
Oh god, I asked them not to come. I just wanted advice!

MICAH
You did the right thing. He came at me.

> TESS

He was—his fists, raised his fists? It was a rage.

> MICAH

I'll talk to them.

> TESS

A rage! He was going to attack you, Micah. For beer. That language, spitting words—I just grabbed the phone.

> MICAH

Tess, you did the right thing. He was two inches from my face — way out of bounds—demanding.

> TESS

He shoved me.

> MICAH

Threatening me, screaming because I wouldn't give him a beer? What was he saying, I have no idea now—break my neck? Was that it, break my neck?

> TESS

He shoved me!

> MICAH

I stood still. I was—I held my ground.

> TESS

Shoved me.

MICAH

Officer?

POLICEMAN
(with a notebook)
He says he's calmed down now. He threatened you, right?

MICAH

Yes.

POLICEMAN

He apologized.

TESS

Good! That's good.

POLICEMAN

He's in the outdoor shower. Is he religious?

TESS

What? Oh. He has—moments.

POLICEMAN

He sounds religious.

MICAH

Jesus stuff?

POLICEMAN

Lotta Jesus. I talked to him outside. Was he drinking?

TESS

Yes! That's what it's about, alcohol.

MICAH

We appreciate your talking to him, officer.

POLICEMAN

So he's religious.

TESS

He's religious.

POLICEMAN

No charges? You're not filing charges?

TESS

That's right.

MICAH

No charges.

POLICEMAN

He was surprised.

TESS

Seeing you?

POLICEMAN

The uniform does that.

MICAH

Of course.

POLICEMAN

It has its effect. He thought I was Jesus for a moment.

TESS

Must be the uniform.

Micah shoots her a look. The policeman heads offstage.

MICAH

Right. That's good. Thank you, officer!
(to himself)
I can't believe this.

TESS

Who can we talk to? Who can we see?

MICAH

We called the police on our son.

TESS

We need advice, Micah.

MICAH

We called the police on him.

LIGHTS SHIFT.

A spot hits Beezie, mike in hand.

BEEZIE

Which brings me back to my brother, you remember him. He says he wants to go to Hawaii—to study.

(a look)

Massage. He heard about a massage school on Hawaii. Right, so he can screw girls and surf. But first he wants to drive to California with these ridiculous pothead morons. So what are they doing? They're letting him go—with cash! Getting him—out-the-house! Why? Because they can't handle him and had to call the police! On their own kid. Excuse me? I'll tell you one thing, if my kid acted out? I mean really crossed the line? I'd think of something, but I would not call the police. On my own kid? The police? Please. Why can't parents get it right? You'd think after years of practice they'd get something right, wouldn't you? I mean they can do their shit—mortgages, bills, surgery, investments, taxes, the responsible adult shit. So why when it comes to us do they constantly fuck up?

(confidentially)

I know. It's because we've taken them by surprise. No, really, I believe this: they totally didn't realize what they were getting into when they decided, you know, "let's start a family!" What is that? It's babies! It's goofy little kids. That's what everybody thinks about—smiling peanuts and happy little toddlers! They don't think: hey, let's have us a really fat boy who reads backwards and an anorexic girl with big zits who blows guys behind the gym. No. They were thinking about goo-goo and ha ha. Not us. Not large, flailing around ex-babies with issues.

(a beat)

It is totally cruel what happens to little children—laughing on the swings one minute and the next minute they're stealing lipsticks and sticking fingers down their throats. And the parents are all

wondering where their sweet, little muffins went. Please. Most
parents either walk away, vanish when their kids start to get too
hairy, you know, or else they keep trying to micromanage their
lives. I heard about this one mother who made a secret lunch date
with her son's ex-boyfriend who'd walked out on the relationship, and she pleaded with him to please go back to buggering her
son. You know, for her sake. Remember: there is no limit to how
low they will stoop to remain in control.

LIGHTS SHIFT

Micah walks up a ramp, turns, looks around. Walks. Stops.

MICAH
(looking for him)
Arky? We need to talk more about your plans. Who are these boys
you want to drive with? Arky? The massage school starts in three
weeks, maybe you should just wait, fly straight to Hawaii from
here, find an apartment.

He waits, listens, looks around, walks, stops.

MICAH
Arky, I'm not sure about this cross-country drive!

*Micah hesitates, then hurries to join Tess downstage in a
pool of light, where they stand close together, tense, concerned.*

THERAPIST VOICE 1

To determine the nature of your son's issues, and potential ther-
apeutic treatment I will ask you some simple questions. Is he
smoking marijuana?

MICAH & TESS

Yes.

THERAPIST VOICE 1

Is he drinking alcohol?

MICAH & TESS

Yes.

THERAPIST VOICE 1

Any other stimulants?

MICAH

Mushrooms?

TESS

We're not sure.

THERAPIST VOICE 1

Will he agree to enter a rehab facility?

MICAH & TESS

No.

THERAPIST VOICE 1

You've got a problem. Four hundred dollars, please. No insurance accepted. Thank you!

They turn to face another unseen therapist.

THERAPIST VOICE 2

Did you use alcohol in your twenties?

MICAH & TESS

Yes.

THERAPIST VOICE 2

Do you still?

MICAH & TESS

Yes.

THERAPIST VOICE 2

Did you use marijuana?

MICAH & TESS

Yes.

THERAPIST VOICE 2

Do you still?

MICAH & TESS

No. No.

                        THERAPIST VOICE 2
Any other drugs or stimulants in your twenties?

                            MICAH
Hash.

                            TESS
Cocaine. LSD. Heroin.
                          (a beat)
And hash.
                          (a beat)
And mushrooms. Am I leaving anything out?

                            MICAH
What else is there?

                        THERAPIST VOICE 2
Still?

                            MICAH
No.

                            TESS
No. But it would help. No.

                        THERAPIST VOICE 2
Were you ever in rehab?

                            MICAH
No.

TESS
(shakes her head)
Cold turkey.

THERAPIST VOICE 2
Are you willing to dig deeply into your own personal lives?

MICAH
That's a strange question for a therapist to ask.

TESS
We want help dealing with our son.

THERAPIST VOICE 2
I believe I can help you. Four hundred dollars, please. No insurance accepted. Thank you!

They turn to face another unseen therapist.

THERAPIST VOICE 3
Do you have other children?

TESS
Two daughters.

MICAH
Two and four years older.

THERAPIST VOICE 3
How are they doing?

MICAH

Okay.

TESS
(simultaneously)

Not well.

> *They look at one another.*

TESS

I think they're angry.

MICAH

One is always angry. She's a comedian.

TESS

But now she's angry about her brother.

MICAH

It's material. She's using it.

TESS

I think they're both terrified.

MICAH

And they blame us.

TESS

Right. Our fault.

THERAPIST VOICE 3

How do you feel about them blaming you?

TESS

It's great to be blamed. We just love it.

THERAPIST VOICE 3

So you're angry, too.

TESS

Is that a question or a statement?

MICAH

It hurts.

THERAPIST VOICE 3

Any history of addiction in your families?

TESS

Yes.

THERAPIST VOICE 3

Mental illness?

MICAH

A cousin. But what's that got to do—

TESS

My brother. Maybe my mother.

THERAPIST VOICE 3

If you had to characterize your marriage would you describe it as
solid, shaky, or crumbling?

TESS

Solid.

MICAH

Solid.

TESS

But we crumble at the kitchen table.

LIGHTS SHIFT

At the kitchen table.

AVA

Quit what? What do you mean, he quit?

MICAH

The school. He left the massage school, never attended classes. Not one. The woman was angry that we sent him.

TESS

But she kept the tuition.

MICAH

Apparently he was rude. Hung around stoned, or drunk all the time.

AVA

Well, where is he? Where did he go?

TESS

Not even a partial refund. She won't refund a penny.

MICAH

He's been calling, cursing at us. He never took the apartment—
curses over the phone.

TESS

He spent all the money. And then he's—vile names to both of us,
for not sending more. Collect calls. Do you know what a collect
call is from Hawaii?

AVA

Would you stop about money!

TESS

No, I won't. It's finite. What we have is finite.

MICAH

We don't know where he is, Ava. One of the islands.

AVA

You've got to find him.

They look at her.

MICAH

And then what? He's not—reasoning.

TESS

He's an alcoholic.

AVA
(a beat)

Rehab! He belongs in rehab.

MICAH

Exactly. Every time he calls we tell him we'll send a plane ticket to a rehab, but no more money. Then I'm addressed as cocksucker, motherfucker, pimp, faggot, asshole, shithead, shitbag, buttwipe. And I hang up. My son. Your mother gets some other names.

A pause.

AVA

Oh, I'm so sorry, Daddy. I'm sorry.
(a beat)

What are we going to do?

MICAH

Wait.

TESS

Drink.

They look at her.

MICAH

Until he agrees to rehab. If he agrees.

LIGHTS SHIFT.

A spot finds Tess. She turns to the audience.

TESS

(sings)

Hello, was there an addict in the house
Were we living with a doper or a drunk
Even a vein-less strung-out skunk
Oh god I hope so, even junk
Because there are dark holes you can't return from
There are dragons you can't slay
Some don't go away
No some will never go away

I've been down and I can tell you
I was lucky I came back
Coke and smack right back on track
You could say—the hard way

A lonely brainy country girl
From a loony, boozy midwest home
Trying not to blame myself
For a son who's stimulant-prone
I couldn't wait to fly away
Do it new, every day
On my own, out to the edge
Out on a ledge, right over the edge

I've been down and I can tell you
I was lucky I came back
Coke and smack right back on track
You could say—the hard way
Now I'm a regular bourgeois mommy
On the American family plan

And I pray my son's a fighter
That he can fight and make a stand
But there are dark holes you can't return from
There are dragons you can't slay
Some don't go away
No some will never go away

LIGHTS SHIFT

A man, PASTOR DAN, mid-forties in a Hawaiian shirt, shorts, sandals and a clerical collar appears on the palm-tree platform. Arky is beside him, shirtless and in shorts staring into the sky.

PASTOR DAN
(on a cellphone)
Aloha! Is this—I'm calling Arky's family? Yes, hello, this is Pastor Dan, on Kulawai. Hello, yes, your son, I'm—I've got Arky here. Right. He's okay, not—maybe a little disoriented, but he's okay. He asked me to call you, so—drugs probably. We get a lotta young people wander into the church, mostly hungry, broke, like Arky. Drugs are rampant—all over the island. Yeah. Yeah, I—usually my wife and I try to fix em up with a good meal, send em on their way, but—there was something about this boy. We both felt— he's—I could tell he's—there's a good soul here. He's good people. And I gotta tell ya, I'm a New Yorker, too. Yeah, Long Island! Middle of the island. Big Mets fan, sure Islanders, Jets—so I'm calling.
(listens)
Well, I'm guessing he belongs in some kinda rehab, you know? Oh you have? Okay, okay, good, good. I hear ya. Yeah, I believe it.

Well, see what you can find—no, no not a problem. Like I said there's something about this boy, we didn't wanna just send him back onto the street, you know? Don't worry, I'll get him to agree. I'm in direct contact with his stomach—he's a big pizza dude, like me. Find a place; we'll get him on a plane. Bye now. God bless you both! Mahalo.

LIGHTS SHIFT

Micah and Tess, energized and up, enter from opposite sides of the stage carrying phones and papers. They keep moving as they speak.

MICAH
There's one in Seattle, drug and alcohol, they'll take him in two days.

TESS
I've got one in San Diego in a week, and they'll accept insurance.

MICAH
Seattle wants the money up front. We'll have to deal with the insurance.

TESS
We can't wait a week, can we?

MICAH
No. Okay, we'll ask Pastor Dan to put him on a plane to Seattle.

TESS

Will they meet him at the airport?

MICAH
(shakes his head)

We'll have to tell him how to get there.

TESS

If he can do that.

MICAH

Big If.

TESS

Big If.

They look at each other, hopeful.

MICAH

But it's a start.

TESS

Get him clean. It's a start.

MICAH

Plenty of kids get off drugs and booze.

TESS

Plenty.

                    MICAH

Turn their lives around.

                     TESS

Right around.

                    MICAH

Plane tickets!

                     TESS

I'll go on line.

                    MICAH

I'm on the insurance.

        They move off in opposite directions.

        LIGHTS SHIFT

        A beam finds Beezie and her microphone.

                    BEEZIE
            (stalks the stage, mike in hand)
This whole country's hooked on hope. One giant hope factory
churning it out—money hope, god hope, health hope, sex hope,
you name it, all ages. Who gets out of bed in the morning without
it? "Oh boy, I hope I have a well-formed bowel movement before
lunch." "Man, I hope I get a hand-job tonight." "Christ, I hope he
notices me at yoga, and I don't fart." And the terrible thing is just
a hint, a glimmer keeps you going. And it's free! Everybody hoping for better than what they got. Especially parents—all parents

are hope-junkies, alright? About their kids. So take a note, a warning: if you have to have children accept the fact that you're gonna
become a junkie, hooked on hope—for life. It's part of the pack-
age: Kiddie-Hope! Really obscene stuff. Who wants to see their
parents running around sucking up to hope? It's so desperate, so
reductive—it makes them—just like everybody else. Hey, "American Parents tonight at nine! Which pathetic couple can hope for
the most for their awful fucking kid!" Listen! Accept what you
have, and deal with it! Soldier on, like I do—No TV spot? So what?
No club dates lined up? So what? No new clothes in a month? So
what? No boyfriend in six months? Screw 'em all. No orgasm in
nine days? Say what??

LIGHTS SHIFT.

*We see Arky alone, shirtless, traipsing slowly (without his
duffle bag) from area to area. He keeps moving as Tess and
Micah come downstage, dancing, carrying a doctor's white
coat on a hanger.*

*They begin a dance-conversation with the white coat. With
each short statement. they pass it back and forth, address-
ing the coat:*

MICAH
Doctor, six months we didn't know where he was.

TESS
Stoned in Hawaii, doctor.

MICAH

Hammered by the sea.

Arky keeps trudging along.

TESS

How long has he been off weed?

MICAH

And alcohol free?

MICAH & TESS

For one full month, doctor, one full month!

MICAH

First a rehab in Seattle.

TESS

But his attitude was wrong.

MICAH

Angry and unresponsive.

Arky stops walking.

TESS

He refused to go along.

MICAH

Their program didn't fit his symptoms.

TESS

And they said he had to leave—so—

Arky starts walking again.

MICAH

We found a different kind of rehab, doctor!

We hear horses neighing. Arky picks up a shovel, looks at it.

TESS

Outside Phoenix, A-Z.

Arky, holding the shovel, hears the horses neighing, looks around.

MICAH

Psychiatrists and horses, doctor.

TESS

Lotsa sunshine, plus—

Arky puts down the shovel, picks up a paint brush and a gallon of paint, stares at a wall . . .

MICAH

Group activities!

TESS

And therapy with stoners just his age! But—

MICAH

He wasn't functioning in your—

Arky raises one leg, keeps it raised.

TESS

Normal, drug-addicted-alcoholic way.

MICAH

Talking total nonsense.

TESS

Staring one-legged into space.

Arky stares.

MICAH

They wanted to commit him in Arizona, doctor.

TESS

A lock-down psychiatric ward. So—

Light drops on Arky.

MICAH

We got him on another plane, and—

TESS

We met that plane!

MICAH & TESS

Doctor, we met that plane!

MICAH

And we drove right here.

TESS

Old Lock-Down, Connecticut.

On the bed platform, Arky sits up in bed.

MICAH

Tell us, is there a diagnosis yet, doctor?

TESS

Doctor, what exactly do you know?

MICAH

Doctor, these drugs you put him on?

TESS

He seems so awfully awfully slow.

MICAH

How long before he recovers?

TESS

When will he be himself again?

MICAH & TESS

Say doctor, can you fix our boy? Tell us, doctor, can you fix our boy?

ARKY
(from bed)
I love you, Mom. I love you, Dad. I love you, Mom. I love you, Dad.

MICAH & TESS
(they blow kisses, wave to him)
Please doctor, will you fix our boy? Askin' doctor, will you fix our boy? Hopin' doctor, can you fix our boy!

A flashy, arms spread Ta-Dah!

ARKY
(from bed)
Mom? Dad?

LIGHTS drop.

END ACT ONE

ACT TWO

The three travelers are on the move again, rolling their luggage, Arky, on his platform kotherni, brings up the rear.

A DOCTOR appears downstage with a large chart. The Travelers stop, watch him.

DOCTOR
(to the audience)

I am the brain doctor. And this is a print-out of your son's brain, enlarged. The print-out is enlarged. We've put him through a battery of tests, tests and scans, did I say scams? Scans. Some with dye. Your son is extremely intelligent. We use a lovely purple dye, and it lights up dysfunctional areas of the brain. It can be quite striking to look at—sections of electric magenta, in fact. And some not. So we are looking for abnormalities, impaired areas, magenta, however small. These were extensive tests. Did I say expensive? Extensive, extensive tests.

(a beat)

The brain is a complex organ. But you know that.

Upstage, the travelers are listening.

DOCTOR

There is a lot of tissue in the brain—the cerebral cortex, arranged in lobes. The lobes are designated by specific locations. For instance, your "frontal lobe" would be here.

(taps his forehead)

And your "sidal lobe" would be here.

(points to his temple)

If you had a "sidal lobe." And your "amygdala," the almond-shaped bundle of gray matter situated mid-brain, is here.

(taps the top of his head)

From upstage, Tess and Micah focus on the doctor. Arky stares into space.

DOCTOR

We are still learning a lot about the brain. I mean, a lot. There was a PBS Special not long ago. The latest experiments, and—findings. Perhaps you DVR'd it. It's also downloadable. Quite downloadable. And, there is a print version.

(smiles)

So what have we found—about your son? And I know you've been hoping for something curable. A Lyme disease psychosis, for instance, is curable with antibiotics, as is syphilis. Something limited to a specific area of the brain that is both treatable, and curable. However, what we have found is—

(a beat)

Global impairment. Massive. Or, a lot of magenta. So—

(a beat)

You lose. You're all fucked.

Arky glares at the doctor.

Slowly, Tess and Micah turn and look at each other, stunned.

LIGHT SHIFTS

Micah steps forward.

MICAH

Here's an experiment that can be done at home. Try to duplicate this: Take a boy, a son—a great kid, big, gorgeous kid, funny, sharp, with a generous heart, an inquisitive mind with a philosophical bent—the existence of god, the meaning of goodness. A graceful athlete, surfer, girls love him, ballplayer, unlimited potential. Unlimited.

(pauses)

Maybe he's a little disorganized, his room's always a mess. Then add some booze, some dope, hey, it's available, he's a kid, an eighteen-year-old alive in the world. Watch him begin to screw up at school, college, get belligerent at home, aggressive.

(pauses)

So. This experiment. Too much booze added, too many drugs? The combination, are they a trigger? For what? What's happening? You try to step in, pull him back, but you can't, his behavior. It's—out of your control now. He won't stop the alcohol, or the weed. Refuses. It's everywhere; he has friends. And then the experiment—his behavior becomes—bizarre. One morning, it's summer, he goes outside in his shorts, no shirt, no shoes, and he takes his surfboard under one arm to the front yard with a large box of aluminum foil in his hand. It's hot—broiling, fly-buzzing hot and you pass him on your way out for the newspaper, and you stop—in your tracks. He's kneeling on the grass, wrapping his surfboard in foil, pulling sheets of it off the roll, covering his board with tin foil.

(pauses)

You stand still. Your mind struggles to grasp what you're seeing, to understand what in the world he is doing. Because it doesn't fit, and he's wasting a lot of aluminum foil. You can't find a place for it. In the world you know there's nothing, no behavioral slot for this action—wrapping a surfboard in tin foil, but you are still open-minded, willing to learn from him—a surfer-dude explanation that will surprise you with its obviousness.

(pauses)

But—and this is happening fast, without knowing it, without accepting, this moment is a moment of terror. You are on the edge, a cave you can't see into, can't penetrate, and what you are about to understand when he answers your question—when you say to him, "Dude, what are you doing?" And he turns to you with his sweet smile and says, "Silver surfing," you understand with the flash of an electric prod to your skull, that what you are witnessing, what drops you to your knees, is madness.

LIGHTS SHIFT

On another platform, Tess stands with Arky in his kotharni.

TESS
(sings)

We go where we're told
The room's freezing cold
Walls creeping with mold
Hello and Welcome to county Social Services!

Babies are crying
The elderly sighing
Everyone's trying
To be seen
To be heard

To be helped

The waiting room's packed
Waiting mothers attack
Waiting children are smacked
Hello and Welcome to county Social Services!

With a smile like an axe
She takes down our facts
And acts like she's done us a favor
Hello and Welcome to county Social Services!

We leave in confusion
I'm in such confusion
It's been a total illusion
To be seen
To be heard
To be helped

Hello and Welcome to county Social Services!

LIGHTS up on the kitchen platform.

Arky, seated, laughs to himself. Tess and Micah are on their feet. Tess hands Arky a glass of water and a pill. He holds them.

TESS

I fell asleep!

> ARKY

When's din?

> TESS

I never fall asleep during the day. The middle of the day? Please take your pill.

> MICAH

What did you find out?

> *Arky takes his pill.*

> TESS

We got home.

> ARKY

When's din?

> TESS

It was—medieval! You've never seen me fall asleep in the afternoon. And I collapsed upstairs.

> MICAH

Never. So—no case manager?

> TESS
> *(to Arky)*

Dinner will be ready soon.

> ARKY

How soon?

MICAH

Half an hour.

ARKY

That's not soon.

MICAH

Dude, your mother's had a long day.

ARKY

I'm hungry.

TESS

I've never been to a place like that.

MICAH

No—advice?

TESS

Advice? It was third world. People in despair, fearful. But they treat everyone equally, like trash. County Social Services! People-garbage tossed into a room.

MICAH

Like—what was his name, in the garbage pail?

TESS

This woman was so—abrupt. Condescending—behind her desk. What did you say?

MICAH

Oscar the Grouch. Remember in the garbage, his head comes up out of the pail?

TESS

This was real.

ARKY

What's for din?

TESS

I was shaking. I had to control myself.

MICAH

We've got an appointment.

TESS

I could've grabbed her—around the neck!

MICAH

For prescriptions, a psychiatric nurse.

TESS

A nurse?

ARKY

What is din?

They both look at him.

MICAH

Pasta. With my special meat sauce.

ARKY

I like that!

LIGHTS SHIFT

A NURSE PRACTITIONER, a tough old bird, conducts an interview with Tess, Micah and Arky. She looks through some papers.

NURSE PRACTITIONER

That's the diagnosis, schizo-affective disorder, correct?

Micah and Tess nod. Arky looks away.

NURSE PRACTITIONER

Seeing a therapist.
                    (waits for him)
Are you seeing the therapist every week?

Arky nods without looking up.

NURSE PRACTITIONER

What meds have you been taking?

MICAH & TESS

Ga-Ga.

                            ARKY
I won't take that anymore, Ga-Ga.

                    NURSE PRACTITIONER
Because?

                            ARKY
I hate it.

                            TESS
He put on a lot of weight with Ga-Ga.

                            ARKY
I won't take it.

                    NURSE PRACTITIONER
You don't have to. It might not be the right medication for you.
We'll find one.

                            ARKY
I don't need anything. There's nothing wrong with me.

                    NURSE PRACTITIONER
You're not functioning.

                            ARKY
Says who?

                            MICAH
Dude.

NURSE PRACTITIONER

Says every report on my desk.

ARKY

It's bullshit.

MICAH & TESS

Arky!

NURSE PRACTITIONER

That's nice.

ARKY

Sorry. I'm sorry.

NURSE PRACTITIONER

Listen, you got a goal here. Get yourself back together. You've had a couple psychotic breaks. You stay on your meds you'll feel better. We'll try Bing-Bong. The side-effects are minimal compared to Ga-Ga.

She hands a prescription to Arky, which he hands to his mother without looking at it.

NURSE PRACTITIONER

See the therapist. We'll meet in a month. You got parents who love you. You got a roof over your head. A lotta young men don't. Appreciate that and take care of yourself.

ARKY

Okay.

MICAH

Sorry for the rudeness.

NURSE PRACTITIONER

Believe me, this was a gentleman.

TESS

Thank you.

NURSE PRACTITIONER

Good luck.
(calls to Arky)
Be nice to your parents, they're human beings!

LIGHT downstage finds Beezie, mike in hand as Micah, Tess, and Arky continue their travels, rolling luggage.

BEEZIE

Guys do not like girls with schizophrenia in the family, okay? It's a turn-off—or maybe a turn-on, which is worse. So I'm getting freaked out by weirdness—I mean there's enough of it on the street.
(a beat)
And what the fuck am I supposed to do about kids? I mean it's in my genes. When do I announce to some imaginary boyfriend that it might not be such a good idea to have an imaginary child? At what point in this—this imaginary relationship do I drop the no-child bomb? Too soon and I'm a neurotic freak. Wait too long, I'm a conniving bitch. Maybe the idea is to just sort of let it leak out, you know? I mean he'll hear about my brother pretty quickly,

then after a while I could, you know, drop pamphlets in the neigh-
borhood, or stuff the mailboxes in his building, or maybe just
leave one of those great mental illness books around that my
mother keeps sending me, open to the page on "reproduction and
family genetics."

(a beat)

Adoption? This is a fact: guys won't admit to it because it's all
about macho ego bullshit, but they are not interested in adoption
because what they want, in their bones, what they want are replicas—little faces like theirs on small bodies. Replicas! It's about
replicas, period! Which is what their mothers crave. Believe me,
I will not go over well with the mother-in-law if I can't supply
those miniature faces. I will become a "Her," if you know what I
mean. Or a "She." As in—"Where's she going now?" Or, "This was
her idea?" Supply a replica, or always and forever become a
"Her."

*Micah and Tess slog along with their rolling luggage, as
LIGHTS SHIFT and Arky joins Beezie, and Ava.*

ARKY

You are my sugar lotus cupcakes.

BEEZIE

Mom and Dad are not going to send you back to Hawaii. You were
homeless there, remember?

AVA

We didn't know where you were. You were on the street.

ARKY

My little cappuccino croissant.

BEEZIE

It's too far! Why don't you at least look at one of these programs?

AVA

They wouldn't suggest a bad place. They've done a lot of research.

ARKY

Never.

AVA

Okay, but I can't have you that far away from me. You can do very well right here.

ARKY

My honeycomb ice-cream sundae sister.

BEEZIE

Just take your meds and you'll get better. You'll be fine. Did you take your meds yet?

ARKY

Yes I did. My delightful semi-sweet sibling.

AVA

You can surf here all winter in your wet suit.

ARKY

They have to.

BEEZIE

No. No they don't. They won't.

ARKY

They will.

BEEZIE

What makes you think that?

ARKY

Because—it's my destiny.

AVA

Hawaii is not your destiny.

ARKY

How do you know what my destiny is?

AVA

How do you?

*He points skyward with a little smile. Getting emotional,
Ava puts her arms around him, hugs him.*

ARKY

Face value.

AVA

Whoa, Bro you've got to get yourself in the shower.

                              BEEZIE
With soap.

                               ARKY
It's a toxic substance.

                              BEEZIE
                              (laughs)
Soap is not toxic!

                               ARKY
You've got to wash them all.

                              BEEZIE
Wash who all?

                               ARKY
The people.

                              BEEZIE
What people?

                               ARKY
Everybody who's going to heaven. You can't get into heaven if
you're dirty. So they've got to be washed.

                              BEEZIE
Then start with a bar of soap.

                               ARKY
By God. In the furnace.

They look at him.

ARKY

There's nothing to worry about, sweethearts. I just say things.

AVA

We know.

ARKY

I love you. I'll get in the shower.

AVA
(as he exits)

I love you, too!

They watch him go.

LIGHTS SHIFT to the kitchen platform.

ARKY

I'm furious. I'm furious and now I ate too much. I had three bowls of cereal and four bananas. I ate too much. I'm furious. Mom, I'm sorry I called you a liar. You're not a liar. I'm sorry!

TESS

Thank you. Okay. Thank you.

ARKY

Dad, I apologized to Mom. I apologized.

> MICAH

Good. Good, that's—that's very mature.

> ARKY

I'll never fall asleep. Now I'll never fall asleep. All I think about's Hawaii. Hawaii all the time! I can live there.

Micah and Tess head up a ramp.

> ARKY

Where are you going?

> TESS

We told you.

> MICAH

A seminar.

> TESS

About schizophrenia. We told you.

> MICAH

We're finding out.

> ARKY

You don't have to do that. I just need to be in Hawaii. I'm fine.

> TESS

We do. We're not.

They keep moving.

Micah stops, turns to the audience.

MICAH

You go about your everyday life—I want to be as factual as possible, you go about your life with your hand caught in a bear trap. And you've got to just—do life: make conversation, go to the cleaners, advise students, pick up the groceries, revise your script, scrape your wife off the floor, while your fingers are being crushed. This is not good for general health.

(a beat)

And, I'm guilty here, I admit it, of being selfish, trying to figure out how to get—some "value" from this inner shredding, turn it into something possibly—what? Enlightening? This construct you have paid or been "comped" to witness, this how-to or how not to, which might—enrich us all.

(a beat)

It's isolating—to have a kid going off the rails. People don't know how to respond to the information; don't know what to say. They mouth-fart. And he doesn't understand why no one calls him back. He keeps reaching for his friends, but they've stop reaching back. Kids can't do it, it's too—difficult, emotional, embarrassing, so they just—they stop. It's easier for them. Their lives roll along—jobs, lovers, accidents, surprises, triumphs, disappointments, accomplishments. And his world—diminishes. Shrinks. Irises down.

(a beat)

And you—gradually you are pushed out—out of the "families with acceptable problems" group. You become "special." A special family.

(a beat)

A few friends, a precious few do try to dig deeper, to make contact. Bless them. But if it's not your paw getting mashed you're
only hearing about pain, or, if you hear too clearly you've got to
close your ears to it. Most people don't get beyond attempted se-
rial-sympathy, because it's too awful, and they've got problems
too—family problems or personal problems: The IRS, high blood
pressure, infidelity, psoriasis.

(a beat)

So I'm trying, I'm—is it foolish to look for—to try make sense of
this—for some "cosmic meaning?" Any? Listen! Hear me.

LIGHTS SHIFT.

Arky's at the kitchen table. Tess is on another platform.

ARKY

I want to go back to Hawaii!

TESS

(sings)

Try living with a giant psychotic
It's heartbreaking, it's scary, chaotic
Rigid then pliant, most often defiant
Try living with a giant psychotic

ARKY

(sings)

I want to go back to Hawaii

TESS

We're haunted by global impairment
We're taunted by dreams of a cure
We're haunted by global impairment
And daunted by what must be endured

ARKY
(sings)

I want to go back to Hawaii

TESS

He went to a job digging ditches
He couldn't dig ditches at all
He went to a job painting houses
Said he can't climb a ladder he'll fall

ARKY
(sings)

I want to go back to Hawaii.

TESS

Reluctant to shower, refuses shampoo
Our house, yes you guessed it, smells like a zoo
Cries then he bellows, we're always to blame
He can't understand why things aren't—the same

ARKY
(sings)

I want to go back to Hawaii.

TESS

He stands at our door demands
Beer, wine, and smores, while a voice in his head
Tells him: crawl into their bed!
Try living with a giant psychotic

ARKY
(sings)

I want to go back to Hawaii

TESS

We're haunted by global impairment
Daunted by what must be endured
We're haunted by global impairment
And taunted by dreams of a cure

LIGHTS SHIFT

Beezie with her mike steps forward.

BEEZIE
(to the audience)

So my friend's mother answered the doorbell. She'd lived in the same apartment maybe forty years, this is an old lady—she answered the door and there was this totally disheveled, ancient-looking woman, Chinese woman, like from the Tang dynasty standing there, plastic suitcase with rope around it. It was dead winter, freezing. My friend's mother had no idea who it was, till the woman—she spoke really lousy English, said her name, "Li Chin, Li Chin," pointing to herself. And her mother sort of gasped —I mean if that's what old people do, maybe she—"blanched," I don't know, because that was their house-keeper's name maybe twenty-rive years ago when my friend was like a toddler, a little kid. They had this live-in, Asian immigrant semi-slave girl. She slept in a tiny cubicle off the kitchen, hardly ever left the apartment even on her days off. For two or three years. Then one day—vanished. Gone. Never heard from again—until she arrived at the door.

(a beat)

She had this desperate, wild-baboon look in her eyes and she told my friend's mother that she wanted to live in her little room again, baby-sit for my friend, clean the house. My friend's mother just—she couldn't believe what she was hearing. She said her husband had died, died years ago, that my friend was a grown person with her own apartment, and the room was used for storage now, and that she couldn't possibly live there. And her mother, she thinks her mother gave the woman some cash. She didn't ask her in. I think she should've asked her in. For a cup of tea. Hot tea? Just to get warm, you know? Come on, warm her up! Tea? Chinese? Right?

(shakes her head)

But she was afraid. It was—way out of her range. And people are afraid of loonies. So she closed the door, because the woman was bonkers, and she was too fucking scared.

(a beat)

Okay, I know this is ridiculous, but suppose she had welcomed her—I don't mean with a banner, but just cleared out the cubicle. And took her in. My friend's mother is this decrepit lady living all alone in a big apartment. They could've—here it comes: cared for each other! Okay, maybe weird, but sort of humane, you know?

(a beat)

So where did she go? What happened to the ancient Chinese lady—with the suitcase? That suitcase! Don't you love it? Just re-member—remember, if you're old and alone and there's a knock on your door and you should see a plastic suitcase tied with rope—open the door wide, and go-make-tea!

In the kitchen, Tess hands Arky a glass of water and a pill. He holds them.

MICAH

You had a hard time in Hawaii. You got—lost.

TESS

You were on the street, Arky. Please take your pill.

ARKY

Now I'm clean.

(takes his pill)

I'm clean now.

MICAH

You've done a good job, an excellent job.

ARKY

It's too cold here. There aren't enough girls here. I can't surf here—the surf sucks here.

TESS

I'm sorry, Hawaii is out of the question. It's too far away.

MICAH

What about California?

TESS

Too far for your sisters, too far for us.

ARKY

You can't control my life.

MICAH

San Diego? Great surf. It's warm.

ARKY

Only Hawaii.

MICAH

This is—how about the Carolinas? Excellent surfing.

TESS

Hey, we could take a trip, drive down there.

ARKY

Only Hawaii.

MICAH

Little trip, have a look?

ARKY

No.

MICAH

Or Florida. Lotta surf—sun all the time.

TESS

You might love Florida.

ARKY
(stomps offstage)
Hawaii! Hawaii! Hawaii! Hawaii! Hawaii!

They look at one another.

MICAH

Hawaii, Hawaii, Hawaii, Hawaii.

TESS

I can't keep—doing this.

MICAH

I know.

TESS

Living like this. I'll put my head in the oven.

MICAH

No room for two.

TESS
(desperate)
Are we bad people, Micah?

MICAH

Hmm?

TESS

Are we? Not wanting him here? His home.

MICAH

He doesn't want to be here, Tess. He won't talk to the therapist, he won't listen.

TESS

I can't bring up programs, health programs, he gets furious if I mention enrolling.

MICAH

He's got to figure things out.

TESS

Alone? The thought of his being alone.

MICAH

To care for himself. We won't be around forever.

TESS

The one bright spot.
                              (a beat)
What would our parents say?

MICAH
                           (considers)
They'd trust us.

(pauses)

He thinks it'll be better—his life—in Hawaii. He might be right. Who knows?

(a beat)

I've got an idea.

                         TESS

I'm listening.

                         MICAH

Hawaii.

        She looks at him.

                         MICAH

On the internet. Some research.

                         TESS

Micah, please.

                         MICAH

We'll check out social services, medical stuff, housing. I'll call Pastor Dan, get his thoughts.

                         TESS

We can't be that far away.

                         MICAH

It'll give us an activity. Forward motion? We need that.

TESS

It's ridiculous! Our friends.

MICAH

It's not ridiculous.

TESS

Yes! Our families—they'll think we're cruel sending him away, getting rid of him, cold-hearted, selfish—Beezie and Ava.

MICAH

Nobody—unless they've been inside this, not even the girls, nobody gets it. They can't. Please listen to me—right now it's the only place he'll consider. He can't be forced into a program somewhere. You've seen what services are like around here.

TESS

It's a fortune—just getting there.

MICAH

We'll check all the numbers. So we can tell him the facts—why we can't let him go so far away. A factual basis for a second choice, choosing a closer place. What's the island, Kulawai, right? K-u-l-a-w-a-i?

TESS

It's six thousand miles away.

MICAH

(nods)

Flights. Housing. Health services. Transportation.

(looks up, a realization)

We've got to embrace this.

                         TESS

What are you talking about?

                         MICAH

What's happening to us!

                         TESS

Micah, you can't embrace a disaster.

                         MICAH

But maybe how you deal with it.

                         TESS

Yes?

                         MICAH

If there's any meaning to all this.

                         TESS

There is no "meaning!"

                         MICAH

But how we deal with it . . .

                         TESS

Life happened. On us. All over us.

MICAH

... how you meet the challenge—isn't that who you are? Really.
Isn't that our "meaning?"

(ironic)

It's our great adventure, you know? Everybody—if they're
lucky—everybody gets one. You just never know what it is until
you're in it. Maybe this is ours. Listen to me, anybody can live a
regular life, with their regular families, regular kids, their regular
fucking problems. Where's the challenge in that?

TESS

Okay, you're having an adventure. I want a drink.

MICAH

Wait! What we have here is awful, deeply, profoundly awful, but
it's ours! And we've got to—to direct it—grab it our way. People
are going to criticize us, yes, and you know what? It's not their
adventure! It's ours, and yes we could screw it up, make a worse
mess of it, but he's our boy. And we do the best we can for him.
Our judgement, the best we can. That's the challenge.

(a beat)

I think that's the challenge. We didn't choose it. We didn't choose
it, but maybe it's an—opportunity. For us. Our "moment."

(looks at her)

Nobody—wants to learn about this stuff—this—a broken mind!
Nobody. But—you do it right, you embrace it. You don't—go on
an adventure half-assed.

(a beat)

So—we focus, decide what's best for him, and—and for us, too, and then we just—do it. Whatever anybody else thinks is irrelevant, they're irrelevant. Fuck 'em! It's not their adventure. Now I want a drink, too, goddammit.

Arky enters.

ARKY

You have to take me to Hawaii.

MICAH
(turns away from him)
Arky, we don't have to take you anywhere.

Arky comes up behind him, slaps a hand around the back of Micah's neck, forcefully holds him.

ARKY

No! You do.

TESS
(shocked)
Arky!

MICAH
(freezes)
Get your hand off me.

TESS

Arky.

ARKY

You do!

TESS

Take your hand off your father.

MICAH
(simultaneously)

Arky, get your hand off me.

ARKY

Kulawai. You have to!

MICAH

Take—your—hand—off—me—now! NOW!

> *A long moment. Arky finally releases him. Micah turns. They face each other, breathing hard.*

TESS

You go upstairs. To your room. Go now. Arky, please. Go.

> *Arky hesitates. He exits angry, upset.*

TESS
(collapses into a chair)

Oh god.

MICAH
(shaken)

Take a deep breath. Deep breath.

TESS

Your face—I got so scared.

MICAH

What, another ten seconds?

TESS

Your face, that look—I've never seen that.

MICAH

Five? Then—wow—I've never felt that. Never felt that.

TESS

Oh god. I thought you were going to explode.

MICAH

One of us. I—I would've—one of us—I think—blast off—would
be dead.

They look at each other—long pause.

TESS

How did you spell it again?

MICAH
(looks at her)

K-u-l-a-w-a-i. Kulawai.

END ACT TWO

ACT THREE

At the airport, Arky with his duffle, wearing his kotherni,
looks off right, edging away from Ava, who is trying to say
goodbye to him.

AVA

So you'll just check it out, just look around, okay? Arky?

ARKY

I won't. I mean, okay.

AVA

And no decisions, it's only a visit, don't make any decisions.

ARKY

They're waving for me.

She takes him by the shoulders.

ARKY
(smiles)

My super-tsunami sister.

AVA

You come back with them, alright?

ARKY

I gotta go.

                        AVA
Arky, do you hear me?

                       ARKY
I'm a little—distracted.

                      BEEZIE
Don't let them talk you into anything.

                       ARKY
                   (looks at her)
I hear you in my dreams, too.

                        AVA
                   (emotional)
You mean the world to me.

         She hugs him.

                       ARKY
I know.

         He turns, heads off right. She watches him go.

LIGHTS SHIFT.

Hawaiian music, Don Ho style. The travelers enter, Arky first, smiling. He's a few steps ahead of his parents. Tess and Micah, rolling luggage, look around, dazed and exhausted. Arky sees someone he recognizes, flashes him the

*special thumb-and-pinkie Hawaiian hand-waggle, a
shaka.*

TESS

It's beautiful here, Arky.

MICAH

Are we off the plane?

TESS

You were certainly right about that, sweetheart.

Arky laughs, it's not apparent why.

MICAH

Are we off the plane yet?

TESS

Yes, we are off the plane.

MICAH

That's good.

ARKY

And isn't it cool that He spoke to me? I mean only once, but it was
definitely Him. He said, "Don't worry!" It was, you know, huge, a
huge voice. Definitely God.
                    (a beat)
Do you believe me?

MICAH

You heard it, Dude.

TESS

Of course we believe you, you heard it.

*An HAWAIIAN WOMAN has entered in a business suit car-
rying a sign that reads, "No Problem." She's smiling. As she
speaks, she circles the three of them.*

HAWAIIAN WOMAN

Aloha! Please come in and please sit down. Of course there are no
lines, there is no bureaucratic wait-time, we don't allow it. Your
son is most welcome to become a resident of Hawaii. Yes, he is
eligible for assisted housing. Yes, he is eligible for disability and
health coverage. Yes, he is eligible for food stamps. And I will as-
sist you with all this nasty paperwork. In life we are faced with
difficulties, and we can help one another survive. It is the right
thing to do. Mahalo!

*She spins around and walks off waving them a shaka as she
exits.*

*Micah and Tess are amazed. Arky, behind them, has both
arms up high over his head, grinning wildly into space.*

TESS

Arky?

He keeps his hands raised.

ARKY

I reached another level.

MICAH

What's going on, Dude?

ARKY
(lowers his arms, smiling)

I'm going to stay here forever.

LIGHTS SHIFT

TESS
(sings)

Here we are on Kulawai
Out on a limb on Kulawai
Wondering how and wondering why
Why Kulawai?

Scrunched up twelve hours
Three-across to the sun
No, not on vacation
It's our son's relocation
Here on Kulawai

Canyons and mountains
Surf's gorgeous in blue
Friendly bureaucrats
And waterfalls, too
Here on Kulawai

So we'll face it together
Rum-punch it alone
Take care of business
Just sad to the bone
Here on Kulawai

Here we are on Kulawai
Out on a limb on Kulawai
Wondering how and wondering why Why Kulawai?

LIGHTS SHIFT

*PASTOR DAN, shorts, sandals, flower shirt and clerical col-
lar, enters with great energy, putting away his cell-phone.*

PASTOR DAN
Arky, aloha! Looking good, bro.

ARKY
(smiles)
Pastor Dan.

They embrace.

PASTOR DAN
Arky's parents, aloha!

MICAH & TESS
(shake hands)
Tess. Micah.

PASTOR DAN

Micah, old testament, okay! Tess, welcome. The boy looks good.
You look healthy, bro. I'm on a short leash today—church dinner
tomorrow evening at six? Can you make it? Meet the congre-
gation? We'll celebrate your return, Arky.

TESS

We'd love to.

MICAH

Thank you.

PASTOR DAN

Excellent! Arky, we got a lot to do, get you all set up, right? How
about a little welcome back Yahweh Shuffle? Jesus is the Light?

*Arky nods, smiles. They start moving side by side (Arky in
his kotherni): hands-above-head, rising up, dropping
down—a finger-snapping shuffle. Tess and Mica look on,
grinning.*

PASTOR DAN & ARKY
(with each rising up . . .)

Ho!
Ho!
Ho!
Ho!

A cellphone rings.

PASTOR DAN
(looks at his cellphone)
Gotta run, folks, archangel calling! See you Thursday night. Ma-halo!

They wave as he trots offstage, talking on his cellphone.

MICAH
Wow, what a good guy.

TESS
He seems like a wonderful friend, Arky.

ARKY
(nods)
He's a little bossy.

He stares off.

MICAH
What is it son, what are you thinking?

ARKY
Surprisingly little.

TESS
Anybody hungry?

ARKY
I need to be in the ocean. I need to.

MICAH

Go for it, dude.

Arky exits.

TESS

We'll be here, sweetheart!

They watch him in the water.

MICAH

Remember laughing?

TESS

Muscles moving around the mouth. I do. And around the eyes.

MICAH

We were good at it.

TESS

Came naturally.

MICAH

Right when we met.

TESS

We even did it in bed.

MICAH

You made me laugh.

                    TESS
A foreign language.

                    MICAH
We were good at that, too.

                    TESS
Any port in a storm.
                    (a beat, watching Arky)
I can feel you taking notes.

                    MICAH
You married a taker of notes.

                    TESS
A full-time who you are.

                    MICAH
You said you found it exciting.

                    TESS
                    (nods)
That was romance.

          A silence.

                    MICAH
It is beautiful here.

                    TESS
He was right. It is.

MICAH

Did you see the smile on his face paddling out?
(looking)
Is he waving? Is that Arky?

TESS

Somebody. Waving or drowning.

LIGHTS SHIFT

Beezie with her mike steps forward.

BEEZIE

Okay, here's a statement I never thought I'd make: I love a lunatic. He's all mine. And I see things a little differently now. So, what is sanity compared to current events?
(pause)
My little brother never combs his hair, or cuts his toe-nails or his finger nails, and absolutely refuses to wash his feet. He won't say why but he's got his own good, nutsy reasons. That's crazy, right? He sits down in the same T-shirt and grody shorts he's had on day and night two weeks straight, eats a pound of dried pineapple, slurps a half-gallon of orange juice followed by a pint of choco-late-banana-swirl ice cream and doesn't know why his stomach hurts. Crazy behavior, right? But if you wear a good tie and a fancy suit, and you lie to start a war—a war!—well, you're dressed right, and you were elected so you must be sane, you were elected! And—it's the sane elected assholes who encourage everybody to carry their guns into the mall, so they can protect themselves from the other citizens with guns in the mall, or they

can go and shoot their math teachers, and their classmates. It's their Right.

(a beat)

Hey, did you know you can miss someone, really ache for someone even if he's standing right in front of you? My brother never used to be scared of anything. A rock. Now the kid's terrified the police are after him, totally panicked. Poor guy hasn't done anything wrong, but he knows they're trying to get him. Non compos mentis, okay? But those macho dudes with the mustaches who want to stone their sisters to death for looking at an unrelated man? Hey, they're sane because they've been stoning their sisters for centuries. That's proven, time-tested sanity!

(a beat)

Okay, so if you see a wild man rushing down the street, arms flapping, eyes spinning around in his head, barking to himself, *but* he's wearing a clean suit and a sharp tie—you know one thing for sure: this man is electable!

LIGHTS SHIFT

Tess is walking beside Arky.

ARKY

I'll surf. I'll surf every day. And sleep.

TESS

What else will you do, sweetheart? I want to help you make a plan.

ARKY

I need flip-flops.

TESS

To fill your day.

ARKY

I need flip-flops.

TESS

There's a lot of part-time work here. I've seen signs.
(waits)
If you think you can.

She waits for a response.

ARKY

Maybe.

TESS

It's a way to meet people, get some spending money.

ARKY

Stop.

She looks at him.

TESS

I'm just concerned about—

ARKY

Stop. I need flip-flops. I can do this.

TESS

I know.

(a beat)

I know you can.

LIGHTS SHIFT.

Micah steps downstage, dressed for the beach.

MICAH

The title of today's lecture is: "What Do the Parents of a Boy with Schizophrenia Need?"

(a beat)

What's necessary? What's acceptable? What's—bearable? Why is it you can walk into any office on this island—bank, health clinic, DMV, housing, and be greeted with politeness, a smile, a direct look in the eye and an actual effort made to help? Why is that? Are they out of the loop? Did they miss the directive to be suspicious and contemptuous of anyone seeking assistance?

(a beat)

Why is a young man who might be—unusual, who laughs at odd moments, talks to himself, get treated with scorn and derision elsewhere but is acknowledged, even accepted here? The answer is: Kulawaiians are genetically more humane than the rest of us because of geographical location, topological uniqueness, low population density, abundance of wild chickens, and no sleet.

He walks into a motel room.

LIGHTS SHIFT

Tess reads, sips a drink as Micah enters, pours a drink, sits.
She doesn't look up.

MICAH

First appointment tomorrow is the housing office. Then what?
(a beat)
Open his bank account? Get a post office box. A state ID. He's got
to do this stuff with us, participate. So he's aware. He can't be
surfing all the time. When do we see the social worker? I wrote it
down, should be in the notebook.
(drinks)
A swim helps.
(looks at her)
A drink helps.
(a beat)
You didn't feel like a swim? How's your book?

TESS
(not looking up)
Who's the woman?

MICAH

The woman? The woman I was talking to on the beach? She's here
with a friend. From Los Angeles.

TESS
You were talking to her yesterday, too.

MICAH
Toluca Lake.

                              TESS
In the water. Standing in the water side by side. Were you peeing
together?

                              MICAH
                          (after a pause)
It was—a distraction. The island, the restaurants, the weather—
just—

                              TESS
Any other distractions?

                              MICAH
Inanities.

                              TESS
Did you tell her your wife was off reading? Your wife was incapacitated? Your wife was grief-stricken, being distracted by rum
and fiction?

                              MICAH
No.

                              TESS
Well, tell her.

                              MICAH
I'm sorry.
                              TESS
Or tell her your wife is "bearing up," bearing up all over you and
everybody she knows.

MICAH

I'll just drink more. I won't talk to anybody.

TESS

To women.

MICAH

Right. To women.
(a beat)
I was looking for a little oblivion myself.

TESS

Well, look elsewhere.

MICAH

I will. I apologize.
(a silence)

TESS

He can't do this.

MICAH

No, he'll be okay in the hostel.

TESS

Function alone.

MICAH

He has money for food.

TESS

He can't do it, Micah! It's too difficult for him.

                    MICAH
He deserves the chance.

                    TESS
It's too complex!

                    MICAH
He'll learn. To be responsible for himself.

                    TESS
All alone? He can't brush his teeth without being told.

                    MICAH
He won't brush his teeth without being told.
                    (a beat)
If we let him he'll stay dependent on us, you know that.

                    TESS
How's he going to manage everything?

                    MICAH
It's a goal.

                    TESS
How?

                    MICAH
He'll figure it out!

TESS

Right. Just raise your voice.

MICAH

Or he won't. And then—we'll come up with something else.

TESS

Another "solution."
                    (a beat)
How about we never see him again?

He looks at her.

TESS

That's a solution, right? Have I said the unspeakable? Rumspeak-
able?

MICAH

We'll figure it out.

TESS

Abandon my child? Am I a terrible person for even thinking that?

MICAH

No.

TESS

Or dies? So he doesn't have to struggle like this!
MICAH

No.

                              TESS
                            (a beat)
For "verbalizing" it?

                             MICAH
That you can say it—rum or no rum, is how—to-the-bone you
are, honest.

        A pause.

                              TESS
                       (raises her glass)
More oblivion, please.

        He takes her glass, turns, then turns back.

                             MICAH
I love you. I've never stopped loving you. Through all this. Only
you.

                              TESS
Sounds like a music cue to me.

        He turns away, starts off.

                              TESS
Micah!

        *He looks around. She rushes to him, embraces him, wraps
        herself into him. After a moment:*

TESS
(sings)

Distracted by rum and fiction
The tide's high
And I'm on my knees
Drowning, I'm not waving
Pour more oblivion, please

Every day he saves me
When I sink and raise the alarms
He comes to my rescue
And I stay afloat in his arms

Heavenly team in loco-motion
Always climbing up some ladder
Speeding somewhere in a car
Mucho wiser, mega sadder
This love that shook the stars

Who does he see when he sees me
That girl in the T-shirt and jeans?
Somehow he's held it together
(We were a show-stopping pair!)
While I've come apart at the seams

Every day he saves me
When I sink and raise the alarms
He comes to my rescue
And I stay afloat in his arms

LIGHTS SHIFT

In a waiting room.

ARKY

I don't like this place. I hate this place.

MICAH

It's a health clinic, Arky.

ARKY

There's nothing wrong with me.

TESS

Okay, they're beckoning you, Arky. The doctor. Your interview. We'll talk to your case manager now. Please go ahead—just speak to him, the doctor.

We watch Arky slog off in his kotherni, unhappy.

Tess and Micah and a young man, SCOTT, about thirty, are conferring.

TESS

He was here doing drugs, homeless.

MICAH

He's a surfer.

SCOTT

He told me. So am I. They matched us up.

MICAH

Really? Well. Matched you up!

TESS

We couldn't even find a case manager at home.

MICAH

Housing is—he's on the list here, but they said it could be a while.

SCOTT

He's at the hostel now?

MICAH

We can afford the hostel—for now.

SCOTT

We might have an opening in a group home. I'll know in a few days.

TESS

A group home—that would be wonderful.

MICAH

Terrific.

TESS

What would—

MICAH

We're leaving on Friday.

TESS

Can we do anything?

SCOTT

He's got to be drug and alcohol free.

MICAH & TESS

He is!

SCOTT

And compliant. Taking his meds. And, of course, willing. It's up to him—to live with other people, disabled people.

MICAH

He doesn't see himself that way.

SCOTT

Not a surprise. You know that, right?

TESS
(nods)

He was—he was a star-child.

MICAH

Smart as a whip.

TESS

He picked up concepts, math concepts—funny, witty, lots of friends, girlfriends.

MICAH

They disappeared.

TESS

Lots and lots of friends.

MICAH

Once they realized.

TESS

Overnight.

SCOTT

Your son has good, positive potential.

They look at him, surprised.

SCOTT

I could sense—a glimpse, who he is. He's pretty hidden right now, but—it could take some time, and work. Hard work from him.

MICAH
(cautiously)

What kind of potential do you see, Scott?

SCOTT

To live a productive life.

A pause.

                              TESS
You think that's—still possible?

                              SCOTT
If he gives himself the chance.

                              MICAH
You mean—

                              SCOTT
Takes his meds, stays away from stimulants. He's not going to
be—who he might've been.

                              TESS
We're not there anymore.

                              MICAH
But a good life?

                              TESS
You think it's—a possibility? Productive—a good life?

    Scott nods.

    LIGHTS SHIFT

    A cell phone rings.

AVA

(answers her phone)

Hey! Okay. Okay. How's it going? Really? It's really pretty? It's beautiful? Wow, that's good—that's—what? How's he doing? He's smiling? Yeah, but you're not going to leave him, right? No, you can't. It's just a visit! You can't. It's too goddam far! Bring him home. Please bring him home? Please!

(seethes, listens)

What? Okay. Put him on.

(upbeat)

Hey, dude! How—it is? Yeah, that's good. Really? You do? Really? Of course. I promise. I will, I promise. Soon. I'll come soon. I love you, too. Bye, sweetheart!

She closes her phone, takes it in.

LIGHTS SHIFT.

Arky and Micah are in a "megastore" holding little, toy plastic shopping carts in their hands. Arky laughs to himself.

Micah glances around the store.

MICAH

This place is enormous.

ARKY

Where's Mom?

                    MICAH
It's like a shopping stadium.
                    (looks for Tess)
Was she wearing a red shirt?

                    ARKY
              (looks at him, pause—)
I hit ropes.

                    MICAH
You what?

                    ARKY
Little League try-out.
                    (flat)
I hit ropes.

                    MICAH
You did! Ropes. One after the other. I was in the stands holding
my breath, you walked up to the plate, the coach starts throwing
to you—whack! Over third. Whack! Over second. Whack! Over
short. Whack! Over third—pulling the ball, one line-drive after
another. Nine years old!

                    ARKY
I remember that.

                    MICAH
And in the middle of it you glance over your shoulder, shoot me
this little look! Then more ropes. I saw them make eye contact,

the coaches: hey, we got one here! I was so excited I—I wanted to cheer.

ARKY

I could hit.

MICAH

You could hit.

ARKY

Where's Mom?

MICAH

What? Oh. She's getting you toothpaste and deodorant.
(a beat)
You can stock up here, once you have an apartment.

ARKY

Tuna fish?

MICAH

Definitely tuna fish.

ARKY

A case? A case of tuna fish?

MICAH

If you need it.

ARKY

What about "want?"

Micah turns, looking for Tess.

ARKY

What if I want a case of tuna fish?

MICAH
(looking off)

I suppose.

ARKY

Maybe we should go to Africa, Dad.

MICAH
(turns to him)

Africa? We just got here.

ARKY

Let's run away to Africa. You and me.

MICAH

What about Mom?

ARKY

Divorce Mom. You can have five wives in Africa.

MICAH
(laughs)

I love Mom, I don't want to divorce her. There she is. She's slipping off into "women's wear"—next thing you know she'll be trying to make herself happy.

He turns to see Arky doing a slow-motion 360°, smiling as he circles, holding up his toy shopping cart.

MICAH
(amused)

What are you doing, Arky?

ARKY
(finished)

My aura.

MICAH

Your aura?

(a beat)

Maybe I should try that.

ARKY
(surprised)

Really?

Micah slowly turns in a circle, holding his toy shopping cart aloft.

When he stops, Arky is grinning broadly. They look at one another.

MICAH

Wanna do one together?

ARKY

Sure.

They do a simultaneous, slo-mo 360° while raising their
toy shopping carts. Tess enters. She watches them finish.

TESS

Okay. So. I got the toothpaste and the deodorant.

MICAH

We just did a simultaneous three-sixty.
(grins)
Our auras.

TESS
(ironic)

Back to the clinic?

MICAH

I reached another level.

She looks at him. He's suddenly washed in emotion.

TESS

Micah? Micah, are you all right?

MICAH

Hug me, please.

She puts her arms around him.

LIGHTS SHIFT to Beezie.

She closes her cell phone, hesitates a moment, turns to the
audience, pulls out a mike.

BEEZIE
(to audience)
Okay, I'm gonna bring up a sore topic. A "sore topic." Ready?
Death. Comic right? Life's evil twin. It's on everybody's tongue,
tip of the tongue, but it never quite makes the whole trip. It's the
elephant in the mouth. And we use these ridiculous euphemisms.
"Passed away," is big.
(slow wave of the arm)
"She passed away." Where? Vague, gauzy elsewhere. Or, "She's no
longer with us." So who is she with now? That's four words, a
whole mouthful of euphemism, no-longer-with-us. And, "She's
gone to a better place." Right, a box underground. Don't forget,
"she passed on." As if the person is still going strong, but just re-
located, you know? Why not, "passed off?" Makes more sense to
me. Or how about, "She's dead!" Says it all, right? Nothing we can
do about it anyway. Dead. And always the other guy, always re-
fers to somebody else, right? The other guy. Can't say it about
ourselves, doesn't quite work.
(a beat)
And in the natural order of things, parents go first. So where will
that leave my brother once they've—passed off? You're lookin' at
her. And my sister, but she's totally irresponsible. It's gonna be
me. Parents have even figured out a way to screw us when they're
dead. They leave obligations, debts, shoes, books, old cashmere
sweaters, pain, and in our case, a whole person. Or, not quite a
whole person. This is where it gets tricky. If I'm making the decisions once they're gone, who can I complain about and blame? I
told you, they're very clever.

(considers)
I see three choices. Since I've been yelling that he's too far away I can move closer to him, to god help me Los Angeles, for instance. Or, maybe I move him closer, say Newark. Or, I just might abandon the nut-job altogether. I mean it's very tempting to just write them off, isn't it, crazy people? They're scary, dirty, embarrassing. We've been doing that for thousands of years. It's acceptable. Used to be you could lock 'em away, wash your hands, get on with your life. But it got: "too costly," too costly to hide them. So the states opened the gates and let 'em out—to mingle—with the "sane" population. Now if you want to "wash your hands of 'em," they're sitting right on the corner with a scrawly, cardboard sign, bent over a heating vent. You gotta walk fast, keep your eyes down, and wash your hands a lot.

(a beat)
So I'm gonna do what always works for me. Procrastinate. Sleep on it. Do nothing. There's no hurry. Hey, maybe I'll pass off before they do! That'll show 'em.

LIGHTS SHIFT

Tess and Micah with their roller luggage, and Arky, empty-handed, wearing kotherni, are close together.

Arky moves downstage. His parents watch him from a platform as he sits, removes his kotherni—shedding his disabilities along with them.

ARKY

(alert, dynamic, to the audience)

Hey, science dudes, get to work out there! This is the me I was supposed to be talking.

(points to his head)

Fix it. I'm waiting, rooting for you, dudes. Stop the coffee break. Make discoveries, advances, I need results! I'll be here, bring it on, take it to me. The next big curl. Get me inside, get me started again, tweak the genome, okay? Alter a chromosome or two, just get me back! Like this, now, unstoppable me! Me, as I should be.

(grins)

Then watch out!

(bounces to his feet)

You know, I used to think I'd major in economics, slip into finance, glide through the markets, make myself a bundle. But what I feel now—finish college—I'll be a little older, but that could be good, right? And I'd like to be a teacher. Get a Masters. You know, I think I'd love to teach little kids, work with kids. All that energy? And they're funny. Little kids are terrific companions. They're—unpredictable. Which is great. Totally. I'm good with that, you know, keep me on my toes. And you get to see them evolve. I mean after they stop crying during juice-time and peeing all over themselves, you get to teach them stuff. Numbers. Alphabet. The whole world, really. Watch small people learn. That would—I think that would be gratifying. And not selfish, you know.

(a beat)

That's the choice everybody makes, right? Selfish or unselfish. Isn't that what it's about? If you're aware of it or not? I think it's better to be aware of it. You'll find out who you are.

(a beat)

And then—start my own family! Once they've figured all this head stuff out, there won't be any chance of me passing it on, right? My parents would love a couple little healthy me's running around, you know? I'd like to give them that.

(a beat)

And a wife. Beautiful, kind, funny—sort of willowy beautiful wonderful girl? Imagine. How sweet would that be!

Manly and graceful, he begins to dance, an exhilarating, amusing, revivifying dance. When he finishes—He grins, waves a shaka to the audience.

As Tess and Micah approach him, Arky puts his platform kotherni back on. He loses the alertness, returning to his slow, damaged self.

During the following scene, they gradually move apart from him.

By the end of the scene, parents and child are separated by a vast distance. (Their dialogue accelerates, becoming rapid.)

TESS

(hugs Arky)

The hostel is paid up for two weeks.

MICAH

You've got to meet with Scott, and see your doctor.

TESS

We'll do it two weeks at a time. They'll take our credit card on the phone.

MICAH

And Susan at the housing office. You've got your mailbox key.

TESS

Scott's looking out for you, Arky.

MICAH

You're on the housing list, they have your mailbox address but you should check in with them anyway.

TESS

Scott and Pastor Dan, too. And the doctor.

MICAH

You can count on them, Arky. We're in touch, we'll be speaking to them.

TESS

Any time.

MICAH

The bank account's in your name.

TESS

And your ID. Keep it safe!

They have moved apart.

ARKY

Did I tell you that I'm Moses?

MICAH

Moses is good. I'm a big Moses fan.

ARKY

A superstar, right?

MICAH

Definitely a superstar in the cosmic religious sense.

ARKY

I'd say in any sense. Moses and Albert Einstein.

MICAH

Don't forget Bruce Springsteen.

ARKY

I won't!

MICAH

I love you.

Further apart now.

TESS

Do you promise to take your pills? Please.

ARKY

I will. But I don't need to.

                    TESS

Don't forget.

                    ARKY

I might. Don't be angry.

                    TESS

We won't be angry. Just remember every morning, brush your
teeth, take your pills.

                    MICAH

And visit your mailbox.

                    TESS

We'll send you things.

                    ARKY

Presents, right?

          Still further apart.

                    TESS

I love you!

                    MICAH

Arky, this is a great—a great chance for you.

                    TESS

We'll visit!

MICAH

Remember, it's where you want to be. Make the most of it.

TESS

Your sisters will, too.

MICAH

You could be in an apartment real soon. Your own apartment!

ARKY

I'm on the list!

MICAH & TESS

You're on the list!

A wide separation now.

MICAH

The card! The food stamp card's in the mail. It's important—check the mail.

TESS

Please take good care of yourself, sweetheart.

MICAH

That's the whole job.

ARKY

I know. I will.

MICAH

Be responsible for yourself now.

TESS

It's all you need to do.

MICAH

There's great support here, Arky.

TESS

Don't lose the cellphone!

ARKY

I might.

A great distance apart.

MICAH

You can see Scott and the doctor any time.

TESS

We'll call you as soon as we get back.

While Tess waits for him up left, Micah turns, rolls his luggage downstage towards the audience.

MICAH

At home, I bike to the beach and stand at the edge of the sea and imagine him on his beach, checking the waves, judging the surf six thousand miles away. At some point every day I reach for him and come up empty. The distance between us, mind and space, grows. You have a little boy, glorious little boy, you hug him and you can't hold onto him. Then you can't reach him. You can't reach him.

(a pause)

And now there's this large, strange person I'm trying to understand, to recognize. And I want—I need to keep loving him!

(a beat)

Two swimmers, father and a son in this endless ocean. He's out there, and he keeps moving away, and I swim out, I keep swimming towards him.

> *He starts upstage, does a slow-motion 360°... then heads towards Tess.*

TESS
(to Arky)
We'll call you from home, sweetheart!

ARKY
I'll be okay—I'm a lucky kid!

MICAH
We'll call you!

> *A pause. They look across a wide expanse.*

ARKY
Do you miss me, Mom?

TESS
(sings)

So I've done what I've done
So I've broken the mold
And my broken boy's here
And my life is on hold

Because this is where he wants to be

Let them think what they think
Let them say what they say
I'll hold up my head
I'll give nothing away

Because I've done the best I can
Can he care for himself
Can he possibly thrive
It's a killer to leave
It's a song to arrive

But somehow I have to let go

When you throw out the dice
 In the family game
If there's one thing you learn
Nothing's ever the same

Nothing except for love, except for love
Nothing except for love
Nothing except for love
Except for love

Arky heads slowly in a different direction from his mother and father, who begin moving again into warm, streaming, golden light.

Micah and Tess stop after a moment, turn towards their son. He stops and looks towards them.

From across a great chasm, Micah and Tess wave to him. Arky waves back.

The LIGHT FADES slowly, and out.

THE END

DESPERADOS

A Play in Three Acts

ACT ONE

A projection screen hangs above the stage. On it now is a watercolor of a handsome, two-story, brown-shingled old house with white trim, an open-air front porch surrounded by flourishing greenery.

In the dark: birds awaken, we can hear distant ocean waves pounding the shore.

LIGHTS come up on an empty platform, raised a few feet above the stage, angled out towards the audience. The platform is the ground floor of the family home. Ramps like tentacles reach from it to smaller platforms indicating other areas in the house, to another dwelling platform, and offstage.

A bench downstage right is angled towards the main plat-form, and a round table with four chairs is downstage left.

Two sisters, AVA & BEEZIE, sit on a bench watching the ac-tion unfold.

Their father MICAH, in a Yankees cap and old shorts, enters with a paint brush and a can of interior semi-gloss white.

MICAH
(to audience)
The great benefit of not having enough cash to constantly hire people is learning to do stuff yourself. You make a pact with an old house when you buy it. The house says it will protect your

family. If you keep it healthy it will reward you with value. If you neglect it, the house will deteriorate and the elements will advance. Of course, you could take good care of it, pay your bills on time, vote, shower daily, be kind and generous and still get fucked over. For instance, with no warning a pipe bursts inside a wall or one of your children gets an incurable, no-escape goddam disease. And that's called bad luck. It happens.

(puts down the brush and paint)

So, turn off your computer, turn on a radio, remember radios? Put on old sneakers and shorts, tune out of your usual routine, and: replace light sockets, repair doorbells. Scrape, sand, and paint every room in the house, two coats! Repair plaster ceilings and walls. Remove dead plaster, fill holes, sand, tape, putty, paint, two coats! Outside shower: crawl under house, remove dead rodents, plumb spring and fall. Aluminum gutters: by hand, muck them out! Exterior trim: climb up two stories on shaky extension ladder, scrape, sand, paint two—one coat!

(looks down, points to a DOG we can't see)

Good boy. Down. Lay down.

(to audience)

Never underestimate instant gratification from physical labor. Your head clears. You return to mind-work refreshed by accomplishment. The house is pleased. The semi-gloss semi-sparkles. Your spouse applauds. You feel like a manly man, a domestic hero. Your children could care less.

Micah starts painting the wall.

(NOTE: The play is constructed so that the actors playing Ava and Beezie can play all subsequent parts.)

The sisters address the audience.

AVA

What happened here
Happened gradually
Happened abruptly
What happened here
A family bending and twisting to adjust
Each one twisting slowly
Bending out of shape

BEEZIE

When we were inside it
Living the years of it
We couldn't tell the cost
Breathing inside a long, bad dream
But we knew we wanted it to be
Someone else's long, bad dream

AVA

People we loved, people we knew
Couldn't really know us anymore
Because you can't get there without being there

BEEZIE

Through it all the house remained
Two stories, attic, bedrooms, family rooms
Basement
The structure remained intact
But it shivered
The house shivered

                          AVA
So—that was history
Now we're wide awake

> *A leaf-blower begins down the street. Traffic noise picks up. A power saw rips the air. It's a cacophony of unwanted sounds.*

> *TESS, Micah's wife, stomps onstage carrying a trowel, wearing a jumpsuit, big headphones, gloves, and a gardening belt. She drops the belt, throws down the gloves and trowel, unzips the jumpsuit and steps out of it. In her underwear, headphones over her ears, with Micah watch-ing, she storms offstage. He turns back to painting.*

> *AVA and BEEZIE, as they were then.*

                        BEEZIE
Let's get them to bring Arky home.

                          AVA
What??

                        BEEZIE
Just for Thanksgiving, bring him home.

                          AVA
No. No way.

                        BEEZIE
So we don't have another shitty, pathetic holiday.

                              AVA

They can't bring him home, Beez. Forget it.

                            BEEZIE

Like three or four days at the most.

                              AVA

Not going to happen.

                            BEEZIE

We'd watch him—

                              AVA

The last visit he ran up and down Main Street shouting he was
Jesus, remember?

                            BEEZIE

We'd stay with him—

                              AVA

Ninety degrees out and—

                            BEEZIE

He was off his meds.

                              AVA

Arky's in a green hoodie and sweatpants telling every stranger he
sees that he's The Lord.

                            BEEZIE

Ava, he was off his meds.

AVA

And we didn't know what he was doing all night stomping around downstairs, broken glass—he drank every beer in the house—nobody slept.

BEEZIE

He's on his meds now, he's stable.

AVA

Right. And he's got to board a plane alone, fly alone, arrive. It's not happening. Call Mom and Dad, see what they say.

BEEZIE
(a pause)
I'd watch him. You wouldn't have to spend any time with him at all.

AVA
(looks at her)
Go fuck yourself, Beezie.

A photo of the house is projected showing a cherry tree in the yard.

Tess returns in slacks, no headphones. She does an angry karate exercise, snapping off punches in the air.

TESS

We have to sell this house, Micah.
(He turns and looks at her)
We have to sell the house. Say something.

                    MICAH
We just put in the air conditioning.

                    TESS
It's made a big difference. It has.

                    MICAH
You said if we got central air.

                    TESS
I know what I said. But it's gotten worse, it's much noisier. The
leaf-blowing, the traffic.

                    MICAH
This is a big weekend.

                    TESS
I can't garden! I'm wearing headphones in my garden.

                    MICAH
                  (sweetly)
It's a great look.

                    TESS
Micah—

                    MICAH
Sorry. I'll re-plaster the dining room. I know I promised.

                    TESS
We don't need all these rooms anymore. We never go into them.

MICAH

So we don't use them.

TESS

The exterior trim is peeling, it's peeling off. The privet is overgrown.

MICAH

I can climb a ladder, Tess.

TESS

Everything is overgrown.

MICAH

We'll prune!

TESS

I don't want you on that ladder!

MICAH

I love to prune. And weed. We'll do it together.

TESS
(trying to stay calm)
It's not—you know it's not just about the exterior. Or the noise.

MICAH

There's joy in pruning.

TESS
(looks at him a moment)
I can't do it anymore, keep living here. It's too painful. I thought
with time—it's too goddam hard.
(He starts to say something)
Micah, please listen: We have to sell the house.

MICAH
(snaps)
I don't "have to" do anything. You wanted central air, we got it,
you wanted the downstairs repainted, I did it. I don't "have to" do
a damn thing. This is my home.

She watches him.

TESS
Can you say what it is, what's keeping you nailed down here?

MICAH
Nailed down?
(bothered)
I don't know exactly. Something is. It's a "mystery."
(a beat)
I can work. I can write. I'm comfortable.

TESS
Inertia is not a reason. It's a condition.

MICAH
Right.

TESS

Will you at least consider the possibility?

MICAH

I don't want to feel—at sea, how's that?

TESS

With an agent, just talk about it?

MICAH
(challenging)

Where will we live?

TESS

Let's get some ideas.

MICAH

Most people know where they're going when they move.

TESS

Well, we know the why, and the where will happen.

MICAH

They move to a place, not from a place. They usually know that when they decide to move, unless they're being shot at—unless they're desperate, unless they're refugees!

TESS
(stressed)

Okay, I'd like to move to Bumblefuck, North Dakota where nobody knows us, where it's too cold to chat, so nobody can ask:

how's the family? How are the girls? How's your son? How's your son? And how is your son doing! But we'll stay nearby, around the corner if you want. And be comfortable.

MICAH

We can always visit Bumblefuck.

TESS

Goddamit Micah, you think I'm kidding about this?

MICAH

And your solution is what? Be a stranger somewhere till the bell rings: Time to die! I won't do it.

TESS

No, I just want out of here. Out of this house. Now.

MICAH

I live here. I'm not running away.

TESS
(long pause)
I wake up . . . this morning I couldn't . . . couldn't catch my breath.
(shaky)
There are too many—echoes—Arky echoes. Micah, I can't wake up here anymore. Too many happy babies. Too much past. I can't, Micah. Please? This morning I couldn't breathe. I'm—finished here.

She looks at him. He's just heard a different tone in her voice.

MICAH

I'd only sell this house for big, big bucks.

TESS

Understood.

MICAH

A dump-truck full, nothing less than a shitload of money. Otherwise—

He shakes his head No.

TESS

So will you agree to talk to an agent. Just a conversation?

MICAH
(no escape)

Okay.

TESS

Good. Here she is.

The REAL ESTATE AGENT races to join them, stands, waits.

TESS
(turns to the audience, upbeat)
We decided after thirty-two years that it was time to move.

MICAH

You decided.

                    TESS
You agreed.

                    MICAH
After you decided.

                    TESS
Okay, that's true.

                    MICAH
Thank you.

                    TESS
We want this to be a kind of chronicle of our move, to help us understand what happened when we decided to leave our family home.

                    MICAH
And maybe help you, too. If you're thinking of moving. But hopefully it's an entertainment. A kind of vaudeville of events.

                    TESS
No. It's a chronicle.

                    MICAH
We're off to a rocky start.

                    TESS
Not surprising.

           She raises a hand in apology to the agent.

TESS
(to audience)

Here are a few questions we've been asking ourselves: At what point does home ownership become less about a possession than a burden?

MICAH
(to audience)

How has what happened here, changed us?

TESS

Robert Frost said home is a place "Where when you have to go there/They have to take you in." But suppose a child frightens his family, do they still have to take him in?

MICAH

Once you've lost the illusion of safety in your own home, will you ever find it again, anywhere?

TESS

Does that "essence" of family that fills the air vanish, evaporate when the family is gone?

MICAH

Can you leave scary visual memories behind, inside four walls? Or will they stick to your brain, like napalm?

TESS

Does the structure of a house, the rooms, the lay-out, affect the structure of a family living inside it?

MICAH

When you finally leave—a prayer? A ceremony? Just shut the door?

TESS

Is an old house like a family—battered, still beautiful, still standing?

MICAH

Or is it just an old fucking house?

A beat.

AGENT
(energized)

Well! For the X-number of dollars you want we will need that unique buyer looking for this great location and—and a vintage house with local charm and history, no swimming pool, a seventies kitchen, sixties bathrooms—but hey, he/she is out there! Somewhere. And it's my job to find her/him. Even if they just want the location and a tear-down.

MICAH

A tear-down?

AGENT

Hey, rich people are strange.
        (suddenly bends, covers her crotch)
You're a very friendly dog! I love large animals.

MICAH
(beckons the dog we can't see)
Just to be clear: We'll only sell for X-number of dollars. Otherwise
we are not selling.

He looks at Tess.

TESS
Right. That's right.

AGENT
Got it! X-number of dollars. It's a healthy number of dollars. As of
right now I'd say that's actually top of the market for a mid-top-
of-the-market location, and a vintage, charming property such as
yours. It's definitely—a starting place!

MICAH
And ending place.

AGENT
Understood!

She returns to the bench.

MICAH
Was she speaking English? It sounded like English.

TESS
(distracted)
Are you calling Arky today or am I? He's expecting a call.

MICAH
(points to himself)
Her eyes lit up when you told her we'd be looking for a new place to live. Did you see her face? Another commission! She started to drool. And she got an erection. No, she did!

TESS
She said we should do a "prep." Prep the house.
(looks around)
There's so much dog hair.

MICAH
Strangers walking around judging.

TESS
People don't like to see bathrobes and pill bottles, clothes piled on a chair.

MICAH
I am not hiding my bathrobe.

TESS
Do you have a bathrobe?

MICAH
I can find one.

TESS
We'll put fresh flowers around and change light bulbs, brighter bulbs, new lamp shades, maybe a few throw pillows and burn some incense.

MICAH

Really tart the place up.

TESS

Whatever it takes.

The sisters, to the audience.

BEEZIE

They arrived with one baby, a dog
Two bent-wood chairs and a maple bed
She was his dream girl
He had his hair

AVA

Beezie and Arky joined us
Three retrievers arrived and departed
They paid off the mortgage
He kept painting the house

BEEZIE

They thought they'd live here forever
Die holding hands in that bed
Part of her's still alive—and kicking
Part of him's still kicking—and dead

AVA

Now the house is on the market and
They'll hold fast for what they're asking
They'll hold their breath
For what they'll net

BEEZIE
Then they'll empty the place together
Year by year, piece by piece
And they'll pull themselves together
And go—go from there, they'll go from there

TESS
(to audience)
Winter, nineteen eighty-three. A snow storm was coming. Micah
kept checking the tires and battery in the car praying the baby
would arrive before the snow. We left the driveway at three in
the morning and drove through every red light—he said if a cop
pulled us over we'd tell him: get us to the hospital, pronto! He was
empowered by fatherhood. The storm came right after the baby,
almost two feet of snow. Our son arrived squawking, carrying on
as if he wanted to go back where he was safe. And he was right.
We brought him home and the girls were over the moon, a
brother! But when I started nursing him the older one ran from
the room and the little one just turned her face into Micah's chest
and sobbed. The world changed for all of us that morning.
(a beat)
He was a gorgeous little boy!

The real estate agent returns.

AGENT
This one is going for less but the pool is in bad shape.

TESS
We don't want a pool. We swim in the ocean.

                                AGENT

That is so healthy! I can show you a great almost-ocean-front
property, but it's listed at twice what you said was your top.

                                 TESS

Then don't show it to me. We can't afford it.

                                AGENT

Remember the ranch this morning that needed some love?
There's a new listing nearby, similar but in better shape and with
half an acre of land.

                                 TESS
                          (shakes her head)

Less land. Or no land. I'm finished with land—just a front door,
maybe a few steps. And a tree. And quiet.

                                AGENT

So—less than half an acre.

                                 TESS

Less than half an acre. And no traffic.

                                AGENT

But you like trees, right? Because there is a wonderful, smallish
cape with amazing trees, dozens and dozens, it's like—like an or-
chard!

                                 TESS
                           (looks at her)

One tree.

Tess exits.

The sisters walk to the bench.

AVA

You ever feel cheated? By Mom and Dad?

BEEZIE

Cheated?

AVA

I mean it's Arky twenty-four seven—

BEEZIE

So you're what, jealous?

AVA

—all their energy, emotional energy. Yeah? It's ridiculous—
"bloom where you're planted," remember Mom always says that?
Now she's trying to micromanage his life thousands of miles
away—she's like obsessed.

BEEZIE
(nods)

I think they figure we're out of the house, leading our own lives.

AVA

Well we are. But—it just sucks. It all sucks. I'm—I could eat a
roast beef sandwich. Serious roast beef—on a roll—dripping
with mayo, real fucking mayo.

                    BEEZIE
                 (looks at her)
You're a vegetarian.

                     AVA
I'm not obsessed with it. Sometimes I crave actual food—like—
from bones.
                   (pause)
You know, guys are going to think our family's weird. And
strange. Weird and strange. It's a problem.

                    BEEZIE
                   (nods)
Everybody's family is a little strange—when you get close.

                     AVA
Yeah, I mean for us. A problem for us.
                  (pauses)
I don't think I'll be a vegetarian that much longer.

         Beezie looks at her.

                     AVA
What? Shut up.

         They return to the bench. Tess has arrived home.

                     TESS
She's wearing me down.

MICAH

There are other agents out there.

TESS

You can't believe the places she's showing me.

MICAH

Why are you even looking now? It's too soon.

TESS

They all have the same listings, just different patter.

MICAH

If you see something you like it'll be gone by the time we find a buyer.

TESS
(looks at cellphone)

I'm getting a text.

MICAH

If we find a buyer.

TESS

Uh oh. She's bringing those short people over again.
(energized)

Battle stations!

They start to rush around straightening up.

                    TESS
There's so much dog hair.
                (calls to him)
I don't have time to vacuum all the goddam dog hair!

> *The BUYERS, taking photos, approach the house crouching, as Tess and Micah hide from them. Bent low like two midget Grouchos, the buyers scurry around as Tess and Micah shift to avoid them. And then they are gone.*

                    TESS
            (sniffing the air—)
Smokers.

                    MICAH
Onions for lunch. And maybe—pickles.

                    TESS
I'll open some windows.

> *She exits.*

                    MICAH
            (to audience)
Chunks of history in this house, this room. Piped in from out-there, lived through right here. Nineteen eighty-nine the TV was a barrel-chested Sony Trinitron and we watched Germans running through wide-open gates hugging and kissing a lot of other Germans. The wall was coming down. The world hadn't seen so many smiling Germans since—Kristallnacht.

(pauses)

Two years later I was upstairs shaving. Tess called me and I came down to see Boris Yeltsin, blind drunk standing on a tank as the Soviet Union, presto, turned back into Russia! An empire became a country before I could get the kids to school.

(pauses)

And we sat on that couch when Bill Clinton took the oath of office, on a bible. Finally, someone our age we could believe in.

(shakes head)

Okay, so it wasn't the first Oval Office sex act, but he didn't lose me forever because of bad judgement. He lost me forever because he forgot who he was. And because he got caught.

Tess re-enters with her cellphone.

> TESS

Micah, they made an offer!

> MICAH
> *(surprised)*

Who, the Grouchos?

> TESS
> *(nods, amazed)*

The shorties. She says they want the house. It was their third visit.

> MICAH
> *(takes her phone)*

A serious offer, ball park?

> *(checks phone, looks at her)*

Ball park.

> TESS

We've got to respond.

> MICAH

Where are we going to live?

The real estate agent reappears.

> AGENT

They love it! They want to put in a sauna. I told you someone weird and rich was out there!

> MICAH

We've got no place to go.

> AGENT

Let's get right back to them. They know you'll only take X-number of dollars. I sense there's no dicking around with these people— they have height issues.

> *(to Micah)*

We will slide you right into a tighter, quieter, expensive new home.

> *(turns to Tess)*

Oh! I just got a listing with a tree, one tree! Call me. One tree!

The agent retreats to the bench.

                    TESS
           (stunned, without conviction)
We can always rent—until we find something. I've seen a few
rentals.

                    MICAH
Live in somebody else's house with all their—bathrobes?

                    TESS
If we have to—as an interim, just until.
                    (pause)
Are you calling him today, or am I?

           Micah points to her.

                    TESS
We'll have to tell him—maybe not right away. Selling the house—
his room?

                    MICAH
We could turn it down.

                    TESS
And hope for another rich weirdo? They met our price.

                    MICAH
It would be a gamble.

                    TESS
I didn't expect an offer this soon.

MICAH

Most offers go nowhere.

TESS

It's X-number of dollars, Micah, just what we told her we wanted.

MICAH
(nods)

A shitload of money. A dump-truck of dollars. A—vomitorium of moolah.

TESS

I'll tell her we'll accept.

MICAH

Wait.

TESS

We've got to respond.

MICAH

Wait! Just—wait.

He paces.

TESS

I always thought—I wanted—that I would die in this house. Get old and die here surrounded by my children, all three. And their children.

MICAH

And me, mention me—surrounded by me!

TESS

Always you. All of us—in one piece.

MICAH

I have to be able to sit in a chair with a book and a beer and a
ballgame on, totally—at home. I need that. My peace of mind—
what's left of it.
                        (looks at her, deep breath)
Okay, sorry. I'll do it. I'll accept.

He takes the cellphone from her, turns upstage.

TESS
                        (to audience)
A while ago, when things started to slip off the tracks for us, everything changed. Except baseball. Right there. Baseball saved us
every night.
                        (points to the couch)
We couldn't wait till game time—tune in, tune ourselves out. We
fell in love with the Yankees on that couch. We got—Jetered! We
weren't big Yankee fans before but something about how Joe
Torre walked out to the mound with his head down and his hands
by his side and the infielders gathered around him—while we
had our arms around our daughters. They loved Derek the most,
but I was crazy about Mariano, his confidence, his smile. Micah
liked Paul O'Neil because he was passionate every minute of the
game, and dropped to his knees on the grass when they won the
Series the day after his father died.

(pauses)

But Derek kept us all watching, even when they lost. He always did something that took our breath away—diving into the stands for a foul ball without slowing down, throwing someone out behind his back, hitting a home run for his three-thousandth hit! His family always there for him.

(pauses)

Baseball got us through some rough nights—chaos all around us, but we could count on getting lost watching inning after inning after inning. We didn't have to think, stand, deal, feel—our nightly escape therapy. Those familiar faces, their little quirks at home plate, their intensity—always with an unknown ending, maybe even a moment of real exhilaration. And we could finally collapse up the stairs and if we got really really lucky—fall asleep.

She hesitates, then does a karate-chop drill.

MICAH

Okay. She'll relay our acceptance.

TESS

Watch out, I might be getting excited.

MICAH
(distracted)

Lawyers, contracts—it could all fall through.
(looks around)

Decades of stuff.

TESS

Or—I might be getting cold feet.

MICAH

We can cover your feet with all the money.

(pauses)

X-number of dollars, wow. I should be thrilled. I mean, X-number of dollars!

(shrugs)

I don't know what I'm feeling.

TESS

Well, even the thought of moving is supposed to be stressful.

MICAH

I believe it.

(shakes his head—)

It's like there's this—this deep crevice right out front—black pit opening all around the house—impossible—to get across. I've got to do it somehow.

TESS

(concerned)

Would it help to see someone, find somebody you could just talk to?

MICAH

(shakes his head No)

Well, if I could find my father in a dream. Hear his voice. That might help.

TESS

Saying what? What could he tell you?

MICAH
(shrugs)

Just his voice.

(thinks)

Or, if I could put them together—with his grandson, and I could enjoy the dream. Watch my father and my son, both healthy, finally meeting.

(points)

Out there, out front, they're sitting under the cherry tree, sitting in the shade. Smiling, talking. I'm not close enough to hear what they're saying but I'm watching them, I'm connected. Both of them smiling, healthy, both healthy! In a dream together.

Tess puts her arms around him.

On the bench.

AVA

I'm sorry, it's our house, too!

BEEZIE

It's like filled with ghosts.

AVA

They can't just—sell it. Okay, they can, but it's really selfish, thoughtless parental bullshit. I mean what about all our stuff?

BEEZIE

Let's call Arky tonight.

AVA
(emotional)
And my room.

(pause)
What? I just sent him something—a muscle shirt, he loves those.
Neon yellow, almost green.

BEEZIE
We'll call together. How long has it been?

AVA
I don't know. I mean, okay we don't live there anymore, but do
we really need to deal with this now? More stress?

BEEZIE
I think it's bigger than just the house. They're trying to move forward.

AVA
Another fucking family issue. I refuse to feel guilty. He shouldn't
be so far away. It's harder for me, I get emotional—I can't hide it.

BEEZIE
How much would you see him if he was closer?

AVA
I just hate flying. It's too stressful.
(looks at her)
A lot. I'd see him a lot, okay?

BEEZIE
(remembering)
Last night—I was in—it was like a small boat and—canoe maybe—and I could see him. He was really out far and he was swimming, swimming towards us. But we kept—we drifted.

AVA
Do I have to hear about your dream? Don't I have enough on my fucking plate?

BEEZIE
And he waved. He waved to us, but we were moving further and further apart.
(pauses)
I tried to paddle to him but—the paddle was—it got soggy, like bread or something. Like a baguette. A wet baguette. We drifted—he kept waving to us.

They stare ahead into the dark. Ava wipes away tears.

LIGHTS drop.

END ACT ONE

ACT TWO

Head shots of four golden retrievers are projected on the
Screen.

TESS
(stops, looks down at the dog we can't see)
Are we confusing you, sweet boy? All the boxes, all this chaos?
(to audience)
A wise woman said you can't know a family until you know its
dogs. We didn't get our guys from a shelter. That's a noble instinct, but if you have a chance to choose beauty, I say grab it. It
helps to be loved every day by a beautiful creature, human or otherwise. Bumper was our first, great with little kids, smart with
big floppy ears, narrow head, and wise as he aged, Solomonic. The
Tank was a poster golden, chunky square head, broad chest, fab-
ulous in the surf, gentle, with the heart of a lion, but short on
brains. He liked to chew the girls' underwear. Koby was third and
when he was five we put him down; he became unstable and
scary. It's not like people—you can't put people out of their misery. It can go on and on and on—and it has to be endured.
(quick look down)
Rory arrived when the ship was taking on water. He saved us,
keeps saving us—the quintessential retriever. There's much to
be said for a good beast by your side. You provide shelter and
warmth, and they supply a different kind of shelter.

The retriever photos fade out.

Tess and Micah sit with the LAWYER.

LAWYER

You should be protected. You must be protected. And you will be protected.

TESS

Well, we want to be protected.

MICAH

Protected from what, exactly?

LAWYER

Contingencies. And from yourselves. We have to assume that the buyers will attempt—through their representation, to wring the milk from your breasts, while the county, state and federal government will try to drain the very pus from your boils. I mean to prevent that.

TESS

Wouldn't it be good to drain the pus?

MICAH

What do you mean, "protect us from ourselves?"

LAWYER

Particularly from you, because you don't really want to sell this house, do you?

MICAH

How did you know that?

TESS
(puzzled)
What kind of lawyer are you? Isn't your specialty real estate?

LAWYER
Real estate and real emotions. I try to get under the hood of every transaction before going forward, so as to prevent breakdowns and any sort of—collapsident, before it happens. And before a closing.
(to Micah)
Now tell me, why are you reluctant to let this house go? You're a writer you must have some insight. Is it some kind of sentimental attachment?

MICAH
Sentimental? No. I don't operate that way.

LAWYER
You're being offered X-number of dollars, so I'm guessing it's not about the money.

MICAH
Not the money. I—haven't figured it out yet.

LAWYER
Well, dig deep, that's your homework.
(pauses)
Going forward, I'll need the original deed, list of capital improvements and all paperwork from when you purchased the house in—

(looks down)

Nineteen eighty-one.

(wistful smile)

Which was the year I was originally seduced by the law. I remember it so well.

As Micah and Tess return home.

TESS

He was a strange lawyer.

MICAH

"Wring the milk from your breasts?"

TESS

(nods)

But I liked him.

MICAH

How come?

TESS

He's sort of a—therapist-psychic-lawyer, kind of—telepathic.

MICAH

This is a house closing.

TESS

(checks watch)

I'm going to my support group and then I have two houses to see. Want to come with?

MICAH
(shakes head No)
We need more boxes. And garbage bags.

She starts off.

MICAH
I don't know how you can stand those meetings—other people's misery.

TESS
Sometimes I leave early.

MICAH
Seeing the faces, hearing all their sad tales week after week. But you keep going—you keep talking to them on the phone.

TESS
When I'm there I don't have to pretend or explain myself, or smile. And—this is pathetic—the really awful horrible stories, the terrifying ones? They make me feel a little better.

MICAH
Take it where you find it.

TESS
Should I be ashamed?

MICAH
Never.

She smiles at him. They look at one another.

TESS

So—how many boxes do we have now?

MICAH

Thirty, forty?
(Indian merchant accent)
"Return what you do not use and become fully reimbursed."

TESS

My movin' man.

She embraces him, a long hug, then heads offstage.

MICAH
(watching her go)

Leave early!

She finger-waves over her shoulder, exits.

MICAH
(to audience, lifting a black trash bag)

See this black trash bag? A thing of beauty. Packing up is work, decisions—heart-spearing decisions. But what's great is just getting rid of shit. As much as you can carry. Be indiscriminate for once in your careful acquisitive life. Stuff, accumulation—years and years of it, years and cheers, years and tears of it—the past— out the door! Show it the door right into the dumpster and breathe! Breathe deeply. The old rowing machine, the fat-ass TV in the basement, the exercycle missing a peddle—lift, tug, lug 'em up and out. Loads of rusty junk—bingo! Get ruthless: your mother's bureau, your uncle's lamp, your father's fishing rods, out. Slam the basement door and for five minutes be a carefree guy. Celebrate what you've created—empty space! Space where there used to be crap you haven't used in years. It's the dumpster song, sing it—the shit-be-gone song of the dumpster! Then button yourself back up, flex the cardboard, and pack up your life.

Tess is at her support group meeting.

WOMAN
My son wants to sleep in the bedroom with me! He gets scared.

MAN
She won't take the pills, refuses.

TESS
(nods)
My son spit them out.

WOMAN
He's twenty years old. He cuts himself, little slices.

MAN
My daughter self-medicates with the booze.

WOMAN
I push the dresser! Block the door at night—I'm—it's—I'm—

MAN

When I toss the liquor bottles, she takes from my wallet and buys more.

WOMAN

I never sleep anymore.

TESS

We called the police, twice—he was threatening us.

WOMAN

I'm of—at night—I'm scared of who this is. This person of mine.

TESS

I felt so awful.

MAN

She refuses help but—how can I put her on the street? I can't do that.

TESS

Our daughters were furious at us but we had to call, we were scared.

WOMAN

My own child.

TESS

He didn't belong in the house anymore. With us.

WOMAN

He flushes all the pills. "I'm fine! No more meds!" Down the drain.

MAN

She can't take care of herself.

WOMAN

He can't control himself.

TESS, MAN, WOMAN
(mantra in unison)

We didn't cause it. We can't cure it. We can't control it. We didn't cause it. We can't cure it. We can't control it.

WOMAN
(a shrug)

So, he'll become homeless, beg on the street.

MAN
(a shrug)

So, she'll get raped, maybe murdered.

TESS
(on her feet)

I'm outta here.

She exits the meeting and meets up with the real estate agent.

AGENT

It's an exclusive!

                                TESS
                              (stops)
A new listing?

                                AGENT
Just in. Your price range, private listing. I haven't even seen it yet.
                        (checks her cellphone)
Oh, but.
                          (shakes her head)
No, maybe not.

                                TESS
Why not?

                                AGENT
                   (still looking at cell, unimpressed)
Well, it's your price range, and quiet, secluded, but there's no ex-
panse, and it's not really private.

                                TESS
I don't get it.

                                AGENT
                          (negative shrug)
It's a co-op.
                      (reads without enthusiasm)
Two-bedroom unit, high ceilings, large loft, skylights, central air,
fireplaces in living room and master bedroom, sliding glass doors
leading out to the woods.

                              TESS
                             (alert)
Really?

                             AGENT
            (sensing interest, low, a conspirator)
I think you'll love it!

            The agent exits. Tess pick up her cellphone.

                              TESS
                         (on cellphone)
It's only a mile away.

                             MICAH
                         (on cellphone)
Tess, is this really necessary? I'm packing.

                              TESS
                         (on cellphone)
I haven't asked you to look at that many houses.

                             MICAH
                         (on cellphone)
I'm in the middle of Updike, Bellow, and Beckett.
                    (looks at book he picks up)
And Winnie The Pooh.

                              TESS
                         (on cellphone)
This place is different.

                    MICAH
                (on cellphone)
Different how?

                     TESS
                (on cellphone)
You'll see.

        She exits.

                    MICAH
                (to audience)
Fifteen years ago, she surprised me one morning, knocked on my
studio door—the phone was off, I was working on a deadline. She
said a plane had just flown into the World Trade Center.
                (shakes head)
The look on her face—I grabbed my jacket and we rushed back
here. She'd left the TV on. We stood right over there and saw the
second plane hit. You want my definition of pornography watch
that tape. The second plane, curving around, approaching the
towers, silent on the screen—slamming, forcing itself into the
building, sliding half-in, half-out. The most sickening sight—we
stood there, the kids were all away at school. I was watching, I
heard myself yelling at the bastards. I don't know how long I
stood there.
                (a beat)
A few months later we saw a helicopter land on a carrier, big
"Mission Accomplished" banner hanging over the deck, and out
popped "W," that lethal jackass, smirking about his "accomp-lish-
ment."

(beat)

Election night two-thousand eight we danced in this room, toasted the country for its vision!

(shakes head)

We should've known, a Black family living in the White House? Way too much for the right-wing nuts to stomach. Now look where we are.

(shakes his head, picks up a book)

The Peloponnesian Wars. Rule one for saving books: toss out the college paperbacks—they're disintegrating.

He tosses the book into a garbage bag.

We're with the sisters.

BEEZIE

They're not really asking for advice.

AVA

But they want our opinions, don't they?

BEEZIE

(shrugs)

They both like the place.

AVA

Mom loves it.

BEEZIE

We should just be supportive.

AVA

I'm sorry, they don't know what they're doing.

BEEZIE

They're escaping.

AVA
(looks at her)
Dad's not. He doesn't want to leave. I can tell.

BEEZIE

He doesn't have a choice.

AVA

Of course he does.

BEEZIE

It's too important. He'll do what she wants.

AVA

Well, it's a stupid-looking place.

BEEZIE

I know.

AVA

Those big white tiles on the floor? It's like a—like a—

BEEZIE

Big bathroom.

AVA

Yeah. So they should keep looking.

BEEZIE

It doesn't matter.

AVA

Of course it matters.

BEEZIE

It doesn't.

AVA

They can't go buying a place we don't agree on, that we don't all like.

BEEZIE

(losing it)

It doesn't matter! We'll never all like anything ever again because it's not all of us! It won't ever be "all of us" again. We can't put it back together. We can't. So it doesn't fucking matter.

AVA

Wow. Emotional.

BEEZIE

Sorry.

AVA

(hesitates)

Ever have—suicidal thoughts? (Beezie looks at her) Just a question.

(a beat)
It's like—I feel shaky most of the time, like really vulnerable? I mean Arky was supposed to be here—protect us from—stuff. Dad's getting old.

BEEZIE
Dad's in good shape.

AVA
Yeah, now.
(a beat)
I thought he was going to become like—this lifeguard, you know? Standing far enough away so I could—but close—in case I really needed help. Needed him.

Beezie puts an arm over Ava's shoulder.

Micah and Tess head to their home.

TESS
(pumped)
Let's make an offer.

MICAH
Really?

TESS
I'm ready. Are you willing to make an offer?

MICAH
Right now?

                              TESS
Yes! It's the only thing we've both liked. You like it, right?
                         (He nods)
So what are we waiting for? We've got to move, we've got a clos-
ing date.

                             MICAH
That could change.

                              TESS
It could.

                             MICAH
Do we like it enough?

                              TESS
I do! It's airy, it's bright. And compact, but not small or tight-feel-
ing. And it's so quiet over there.
                       (looks at him)
If you're not sure we can make another visit. I don't want to push
you.

                             MICAH
                      (shakes head No)
I've seen it.
                     (beat, decisively)
Call the agent. Then what, she calls the owner's agent?

TESS
(nods, about to call)

You know, this could be a nightmare—coordination, timing? We need the money from selling the house to buy this co-op but our stuff has to be out of the house, and we can't put it in the co-op because we won't own it yet!

MICAH

Easy, easy girl.

TESS

So we'll have to put everything in storage for what, a couple days?

MICAH

Tess, we haven't even made an offer.

TESS

It's ridiculous!

MICAH

You might be putting your anxiety—the cart of your anxiety, before the horse of our moving.

He smiles. She shoots him a look.

TESS
(nods, exhales)

Okay. Right, thanks. You're right.
         (punches a number into her cellphone)
I'll calm down.

> *Tess and Micah are on the phone with their real estate*
> *agent, who is also on the phone with the Seller's AGENT.*

TESS
(into phone)
We want to make an offer on the co-op: Z-number of dollars.

(NOTE: The following is speeded up, double-time.)

AGENT
(on phone)
Okay, Z is a good starting point.
> *(picks up a second cellphone, calls agent 2)*
Tess and Micah are offering Z-number of dollars for the co-op.

AGENT 2
(on two cellphones, to her client)
I've got an offer of Z-number of dollars on your co-op.
> *(a beat, then into other phone)*
She'll come down Y.
> *(on phone to Tess)*
She'll come down Y.

TESS
(on phone)
Only Y? That's all she'll come down?
> *(looks at Micah, points upwards, he nods, then into phone)*
Offer Z plus.

> AGENT
> *(on phone to agent 2)*

Z plus.

> AGENT 2
> *(on phone to client)*

Z plus.
> *(listens, then on phone to agent)*

She'll come down Y more.

> AGENT
> *(on phone to Tess)*

She's only down Y more.

> TESS
> *(on phone)*

Y more? She's hardly moving.
> *(points upwards, Micah nods reluctantly, on phone to agent)*

Okay, Z plus plus.

> AGENT
> *(on phone to agent 2)*

We're up to Z plus plus.

> AGENT 2
> *(on phone to client)*

Z plus plus.
> *(listens, then on phone to agent)*

Holding firm. We're not coming down.

AGENT
(on phone to Tess)

No retreat.

TESS
(on phone to agent)

Hold on.
(to Micah)

She's not budging.
(Micah shakes his head No)

Agreed. Plus plus plus is too much.
(he nods)

I know, but—suppose.

MICAH
(starts off)

Let's go.

TESS

Just wait, I'm figuring something.

He starts moving away.

MICAH

Tess, we are not giving in to this.

TESS

Listen to what I'm thinking, Micah—wait—halt!
(a beat)

We'll have to rent a house, and storage space. It will cost us more than another "plus" to her—if she'll bite.

MICAH

Bite?? You're ready to offer her plus plus plus?

TESS

It's logical. Why not overpay for what we want now, than spend it on a rental and still be looking?

MICAH
(comes back to her)
You always try to confuse me with logic.

TESS
(grins)
 Our final offer?
(He nods, then into phone)
Okay, Z plus plus plus!

AGENT
(on phone to Agent 2)
We are now at Z plus plus plus. Will she accept our offer?

AGENT 2
(on phone to client)
Z plus plus plus.
(listens, then on phone to agent)
Yes. We're good for Z plus plus plus.

AGENT
(on phone to Tess)
Congratulations! Z plus plus plus it is.

                              TESS
                            (to Micah)
The bitch accepted!

              They look at one another, stunned.

                          TESS & MICAH
Plus plus plus.

                              TESS
                            (excited)
I can't believe it.
              (throws her arms around him, they embrace)
We've got so much to do!
                    (He's staring off into space)
We'll make lists. We'll need lists. A lot of lists!
                        (looks at him)
Micah, you're okay with it. Are you sure?

                             MICAH
                            (nods)
Feels strange buying a place Arky's never seen. Are you calling
him today, or am I?

              She points to him.

                              TESS
Two bedrooms and a loft. You think there's a How-To-Downsize
book? Must be, right? I better go on line.

              As they move to the round table.

MICAH

You really told me to "halt."

TESS
(nods)
It was a focus moment, the negotiation was heading south.

They sit down with their lawyer.

LAWYER
(looks at papers)
Well, isn't this delicious! Two closings back to back—entangled, problematical.

TESS

We're not sure how to handle all the—

LAWYER

Stop! That's why you hired me. Down payments, escrow accounts, engineer's report, closing dates, closing costs, cutting checks, depositing checks, seller's agent, seller's attorney, buyer's agent, buyer's attorney—it's a jungle out there and I'm your Tarzan! I swing through the forest of complexity. Every obstacle in our path will be overcome.
(to Micah)
And have you done your homework?

MICAH
(shakes his head No)
I'm—I can't quite get a hold.

LAWYER

Not good enough! You've obviously agreed to sell your house and move. But that's just a physical, monetary reality. It's not moving forward, it's not charging ahead with your life. Am I clear? What's your reluctance? What's stopping you?

MICAH

I don't know! My reluctance to leave the house—I'll keep look-ing—for the why.

LAWYER

Good. I cherish clarity. In fact, I put a high premium on clarity.

TESS

We're getting anxious about all the details, the dates.

LAWYER

"We," or you?

TESS

Me! It's me. Totally me.

LAWYER
(looks at her)

You harbor a lot of anger.

TESS
(surprised, glances at Micah, who shrugs)

Well, maybe I do.

LAWYER

It's like a hump on your back.

TESS

It is? A hump?

(Micah nods, she looks at him.)

LAWYER

Just a metaphor. Do you know what it's about, this anger?

TESS

(hesitates)

I do. Yes.

LAWYER

Good. Once a day.

(spreads his fingers)

This much potato vodka. At eight p.m.

(shrugs)

Six p.m. Let me verbalize one more perhaps evident nonetheless trenchant consideration: All of what we do here is not about the selling or buying of property.

(smiles)

I run a full-human-service operation—which reminds me, going forward?

(sticks out his hand)

I'll need a few more rubles.

Micah and Tess head for home.

                            TESS
                          (agitated)
We've got to really pare down. There's way too much furniture,
rugs, lamps—We'll need to have an estate sale.

                Micah shakes his head No.

                            TESS
Micah, we're going from a two-story house with a basement, an
attic.

                           MICAH
I'm aware of it. No "estate" sale.

                            TESS
Why not?

                           MICAH
The idea of people weaseling around inside my house nauseates
me. I don't know how anybody does it.

                            TESS
So we'll do it outside, a yard sale. That's what people do when
they move. They have yard sales, garage sales.

                           MICAH
Not me. I don't want strangers in my yard.

                            TESS
We don't even have to be there.

                    MICAH
Doesn't matter.

                    TESS
We hire a company to do it. They take a commission.

                    MICAH
No.

                    TESS
We can go to the movies!

                    MICAH
                   (adamant)
It's not going to happen.

                    TESS
It's cash.

                    MICAH
We'll give stuff away.

                    TESS
For our trash—hundreds and hundreds of dollars. What's the big
fucking deal?

                    MICAH
Nobody is evaluating our belongings, our history.

TESS

We evaluate, we put the price tags on.

MICAH

Nobody! You understand me??

He moves away, she snaps off a karate punch.

TESS

Who made you "the decider"?

MICAH

(stops, turns)

Me. I'm deciding for me. You want an "estate" sale? Okay, great, be my guest. I'll rent a chain saw: And we can cut everything in half! Half a couch, half a table, half a bed—cash for your trash— all yours! See what you get.

TESS

(builds to a crash)

Oh! OH! You think—you think you're so Mr. Macho, just go off and do work: pack boxes, carry, lug stuff, drive to the dump—be- cause—because you're "the man." And you let me—leave me all the details, the goddam details—phone calls, contacts, de-cisions, the timing—all the fucking worrying! You never worry! All the worrying to me! Well I've had it, I'm done, I've had enough. I've had enough of this—all of this! I've had it, I've had enough! And you never ever worry! You don't—you don't worry—I do it for both of us—all the time! I worry all the time about everything! All the fucking time—and you never—worry.

He comes back to her.

MICAH
(puts his arms around her)
You know, maybe we should be drinking more. All this com-mo-tion—we've ignored our drinking.
(pause)
I won't destroy the furniture.

TESS
(regrouping)
I know.

MICAH
And I'll do some more worrying.

TESS
Thank you.

The sisters, to the audience.

AVA
What they fight about
Is not what they fight about
They don't care about rugs
Or couches
Or small wooden tables against the wall
Or even cash
Well, maybe a little about cash

BEEZIE

They are fighting about loss
A river they can't see
But they can feel something
It's in the house
They're standing in the river
And they know they have to leave
It's rising
She has to get him out

Tess gets a call from a woman in her support group.

TESS
(on cellphone)

It sounds like she should be hospitalized. I've got two numbers for you to call. I'll text them.
(listens)
No. Just—you're a strong, resilient woman. You can get through this—you're not alone. Okay, let me know. You can call later. Bye now.

MICAH

Half-strangers with big problems?
(Tess nods)
You deserve combat pay.

TESS
(shakes her head, changing the subject)
I've decided to divest—all my gardening tools—out.

MICAH

Really?

TESS

First come, first served. I'll spread them on the driveway. I e-mailed my friends.

MICAH

You love to garden.

TESS
(looks at her hands)
My hands are complaining, they can't take it.

MICAH
(ruefully)
So—no more obscene, foot-long zucchini?

TESS
(ironic)
I'll become an ex-gardener. Maybe I'll "consult."

MICAH

You know, I hardly ever listen to my vinyl anymore but I can't throw out these records. I bought some of them in high school—Clifford Brown, MJQ, Mildred Bailey.
(looks at her)
Down-size stuff doesn't mean down-size your life.

TESS

Well, I think it's more like tighten focus.

MICAH

Tighten focus on what?

TESS
(decisively)

I'm going to get an electric piano.
(points)
This one's too big for the co-op.

MICAH
(surprised)

Your piano?

TESS
(suddenly distressed)

It's too big! We've got to scale back, make choices.

MICAH
(looks into a box)

I guess, but—how can I throw out my father's typewriter? Or my mother's law degree? I can't do it.

TESS

What about her—art work?

MICAH

The watercolors? Really?

TESS

They take up a lot of space.

(a beat)

We can't sentimentalize objects, Micah. We've got to move forward.

(pulls out a list)

So from the garage we should lose the old kayak, bicycles, baseball bats, all the interesting driftwood—and the hubcaps.

MICAH

(bothered, a beat)

Oh, okay. So from the attic—we can lose the doll house, little ice
skates, rocking horse, the highchair your father built, and the
crib?

She shoots him a look. Tess exits.

The ARCHITECT enters.

ARCHITECT

(an air of British condescension)

Well, they asked me to come by, take a peek, maybe sketch out a
few concepts.

MICAH

We got the message. Sure, come on in—watch the boxes.

*The Architect looks around, suddenly covers his crotch
from the dog we don't see.*

ARCHITECT

(not pleased)

Super friendly dog.

> MICAH

Sorry.

> *(snaps his fingers for the dog)*

What sort of architectural work are they thinking of doing?

> ARCHITECT

> *(starts sketching)*

Well—they've developed some—interesting notions.

> MICAH

Oh?

> ARCHITECT

> *(not looking at Micah)*

Grand old girl, this house. I walked around outside. Wonderful look. You've been here a while, have you?

> MICAH

Thirty plus.

> ARCHITECT

So I told them the trick is to maintain the integrity of the original design—this splendid traditional structure, while ripping out the guts, the dated guts of the inner space—the spatial guts.

> MICAH

> *(surprised)*

That's what they want to do?

ARCHITECT
(nods)
They love the location and the classic silhouette.

MICAH

So, upstairs, too?

ARCHITECT
Right down to the studs. Every square inch of it.

MICAH
(a beat)
And how does that "maintain the integrity of the original design?"

ARCHITECT
(shrugs)
Well—they know what they want. Clean, modernist interior, traditional cedar shakes exterior. And a pool.
                    (looks at Micah)
They're pool people.

MICAH

How did I know that?

Tess and her ELDERLY RELATIVE visit the new co-op.

ELDERLY RELATIVE
Well, look at this! When do you close, dear?

TESS
Soon. Too soon. First we close on the house.

ELDERLY RELATIVE
(confidentially)
You know, your mother was never comfortable that you left the city and moved out here.

TESS
I know that.

ELDERLY RELATIVE
She used to call me and cry. I'm telling you this as your dearest and closest relation.
(Tess nods)
She felt abandoned.
(Tess says nothing)
Well, isn't this exciting! After all you've been through there is nothing like a fresh start!

TESS
It feels right.

ELDERLY RELATIVE
And the size. Smaller, newer, quieter. Not too small is it, the one extra bedroom?

TESS
No, I don't think—

ELDERLY RELATIVE
In case—someone ever comes—back?

TESS
(glances at her)
We'll have a couch in the loft, for surprises.

ELDERLY RELATIVE
Perfect. Have you told the girls, have they seen it? Of course they have.

TESS
They pretend to like it.

ELDERLY RELATIVE
They'll get over it.
(low, sad voice)
And how are things going with your—difficulties?

TESS
(shoots her a look)
We call. Arky knows we're moving.

ELDERLY RELATIVE
I don't know how you do it—and from so far away. I'd have to have him near me. Right at home so I could care for him myself.
(she turns around as Tess seethes)
But you know best, you know best.

TESS
(her inner unheard voice)
Yes, we do, you shithead. You vicious, ignorant, judgmental old twat. You think proximity is a cure? You have no idea, not a clue.

What do you know about our lives, about his illness, about how we deal with anything?

ELDERLY RELATIVE
(not hearing it, her back to Tess)

Should we get a latte? Do you have time?

Tess does a few karate chops.

TESS
(to audience)

We speak to shrinks, "specialists," read the literature—the big hope seems to be when they finally pinpoint the "screwy" gene—and kind of yank on it—then presto!

ELDERLY RELATIVE
(her back to Tess)

Have you met the neighbors? What have you heard about them?

TESS
(to audience)

People love scandal stories, catastrophes, sex and money stories, but there's one thing nobody wants to hear about: mental illness. They duck and run.

(hands over her ears)

"Stop! Stop, no information, no facts! We have our own problems." Crazy is an amazing turn-off. It's medieval how threatened people get. They'd rather you just shut it away in the attic and not mention it, "that thing you've got wrong in your life." Or, they'll make an unspoken pact—you keep the anguish and pain to yourself and we'll promise to make a token inquiry, "how's that thing in the attic going?" And you just give a shrug, and they'll do their sad head-shake side to side, belch out a platitude or some inane suggestion and then it's on to who's screwing whose ex-sister-in-law.

                    ELDERLY RELATIVE
Look at this view—I know you'll be so happy here!

                         TESS
                  (inner unheard voice)
Will I? A happy bumper-sticker mom? "My Child is a Student at Happy Face Middle School!" "My Child Plays Flute at Genius High!" I'd like to flash a couple at them: "My Child Never Smiles!" "My Child Is in Lock-Down at Psych-Ward State!"

                    ELDERLY RELATIVE
                    (not hearing it)
It's so tranquil and so verdant.

                         TESS
                    (to audience)
This ignorance has been going on for centuries. But until you live around it you have no idea how alone you can be made to feel. And responsible. And ashamed. And—hateful.

                    ELDERLY RELATIVE
                (turns to her, lowers voice—)
Oh, did you hear about Greg's sister—and the pharmacist? I hesitate to bring it up.

    Micah is still packing.

MICAH
(to audience)

Add it up, thousands of days and nights, events lived through together—blizzards, elections, birthday parties, Super Bowls, hurricanes, Final Fours, recitals, graduations, World Series, mass shootings, Academy Awards, births, opening nights, loved ones gone to ground. And all the good mornings—how did you sleep, any dreams? Kissing each other good night, good night, good night, good night. Family history weighs a ton—this house of memory.

(looks around)

Empty closets, bookshelves—everything in pieces. It's like when the kids left home, the ritual break-away, naturally aging out of the house. But if one leaves home—abruptly, unnaturally—for reasons you couldn't possibly anticipate, it sends out a tremor, a tectonic tremor that shakes everybody, rattles that sense of safety you've created together. It's like a seismic wave rolls over the family.

(a beat)

A teenage boy loses competence, loses his way, struggles to understand, to comprehend and just stay a-fucking-float. This—if you saw him on the street—a—just a large ruin of a person now, you'd steer clear, you would. But I see a young man fighting a great battle, a constant battle. And I'm realizing—hey, what he has to do to get through a day? Every day. Compared to the rest of us? It's heroic.

A beat as he goes back to packing.

                         TESS
                 (moving down the ramp)
The dumpster's almost full again. What did we decide about the
wicker chair? I think I'll give it away. You okay with that? The
wicker chair?

                 He nods.

                         TESS
Oh, the cleaning service is calling back and we need bubble wrap
for the photos and the chachkas. Are you calling Arky today or am
I?

                         MICAH
I am.

                         TESS
              (stops on ramp, looks around)
Wow, empty bookshelves. We must really be moving.

                 Micah passes carrying a box.

                         TESS
Did you see what the co-op board wants to know about us, all that
financial stuff, the numbers, the details? It's intrusive.

                         MICAH
And five personal recommendations. We're being seriously
scoped.

TESS

Can they really ask so many intimate questions—see everything we've got?

MICAH

They can ask whatever they want. The good thing is when they're all done looking I won't need my colonoscopy.
(remembering)
Oh—where's the ladder? Did you move the ladder?

TESS

I gave it away.

He's not happy.

TESS

There won't be any room for it over there.

MICAH

You gave away my ladder?

TESS

Technically it was my ladder. It was a gardening ladder, for pruning.

MICAH

It was the house ladder, for the house.

TESS

Jan and Frank got excited, they were about to go buy one.

MICAH

Oh, that's great. Now we can go buy one.

TESS

I don't think we'll need a ladder.

MICAH
(bothered)

Anything else I should know about—missing?

TESS

The big shovel. And I'd like to get rid of the charcoal grill, it's filthy.

MICAH
(turns and moves off)

Don't.

TESS
(calling after him)

It's filthy and there's no room for it!

> She stomps her feet in frustration, maybe does a karate chop. As she starts down the ramp she stops, pulls out her cellphone.

> The sisters are on the phone with their mother.

BEEZIE
(on cellphone)

Mom.

                              AVA
            (on cellphone, simultaneously displeased)
Mom.

                              TESS
                       (on cellphone)
I know you're both very busy, but decisions have to made about
your things.

                              AVA
                       (on cellphone)
Just lose them!

                             BEEZIE
                       (on cellphone)
Don't throw them out!

                              TESS
                       (on cellphone)
Next weekend, please.

                              AVA
                       (on cellphone)
Mom, no way. I have so much.

                             BEEZIE
                       (on cellphone)
I'm way behind on my reports.

TESS
(on cellphone)
Stop. We need your help. As in help.
(ending the call)
I love you both.

AVA
(on cellphone, glum)
Love you.

BEEZIE
(on cellphone, glum)
Love you.

They look at one another, then look towards the platform.

AVA
I will not carry things.

BEEZIE
I think they just want moral support.

AVA
We can give that on the phone. They want physical support—we show up and "pitch in" then that's proof, that's our "approval."

BEEZIE
And a lot of hugging.

AVA
Yeah, it's like who's the adult?

Beezie starts to rise.

                          AVA

Wait.

                        BEEZIE
                        (stops)

What up?

                          AVA
                       (hesitates)

I think I'm—scared.

                        BEEZIE

Scared of what?

                          AVA

I'm not sure. The house. Seeing it? Empty. Naked. Like—un-
dressed?

        They look at one another.

        Micah is back at the house.

                        MICAH

When we get off the plane for a visit, all our son wants is to be
driven around, and to eat. No conversation. Can't hug him, can't
kiss him, refuses to be touched. Won't allow it. Germs. So we drive
around, watch him eat, drop him off. Then we go drink. Next day
we drive around, drive around, watch him eat, drop him off and
go drink. The next day we drive around, drive around, watch him

eat, and go drink. And drink and drink and drink and drink ourselves into fucking oblivion.

He heads off.

The sisters arrive home.

                          BEEZIE
Mom!

                           AVA
Dad?

                     BEEZIE & AVA
We're home!

                          TESS
          (embraces them, opens carton, amused)
Who wants Paddington Bear? Cabbage Patch dolls?

                           AVA
Oh god.

                         BEEZIE
                       (reaching)
My Cabbage Patch.

                          TESS
A kitchen sink? Cash "rooster"?

                              AVA
Mom, people collect these.

                            BEEZIE
We could sell them on eBay, Mom.

                             TESS
You could.
                    (holds up hand puppet)
Remember these?

                            BEEZIE
                    (reaches for one)
I was the waitress.

                              AVA
No, I was the waitress. You were the cook. You wanted to be the
waitress.

                            BEEZIE
Right. I hated being the cook stuck in the kitchen. I wanted to be
out front where the action was.

                              AVA
You've got to save this stuff, Mom.

                            BEEZIE
                    (tearing up)
This is so ridiculous.

> TESS
> *(puts an arm around Beezie)*

I've been saving it. We've got no room.

> AVA

So let's put it in storage.

> TESS

No storage. We just got permission to move our things right into the co-op before closing.

> AVA

So it's all going in the dumpster?

> TESS

Better take what you want now.

> BEEZIE
> *(reaching into box)*

Hey, the ukulele.

She strums, tunes it.

> AVA
> *(looking around)*

God, this is so weird. How can you do it?

> TESS

I keep my head down and fill boxes. But it's getting spooky. And your father's in a daze.

                              AVA
Totally spooky.

                             BEEZIE
                           (strumming)
What's he in a daze about?

                              TESS
Leaving.

                             BEEZIE
We're all in a daze.

                              AVA
Yeah, like—like we're the Daze family.

                              TESS
Well, he's having a hard time figuring it out—emotionally.

                              AVA
Hey, this house right now?

                             BEEZIE
It's chaos.

                              AVA
It's like looking at a skeleton of somebody really really familiar—
like Elvis.
                            (pause)
Or Shakespeare.

TESS
(nods)
Sometimes I feel embarrassed for the house.

BEEZIE
(starts to play and sing)
"Washington at Valley Forge Freezing cold but up spoke George
singing' Vo-doe-de-o, vo-doe-de-o-doe. . . .

*Tess and Ava, grinning, join in trading lines and gestures
the way they did it years ago*

TESS, SISTERS
"On his ukulele, daily
He would strum
Beedle um bum
Dancing, prancing
And then he'd holler Red Hot Mama!

Crazy words, crazy tune
All that George could croon and moon
Was voe-do-de-o, voe-do-de-o-doe"

They end laughing as Micah enters carrying a box

MICAH
Angel voices to the rescue!

BEEZIE
(starts to strum)
Dad?

MICAH
(points to her)
Look at that—the fingers never forget!
(sings)
"Yes sir, that's my baby No sir, I don't mean maybe Yes sir, that's
my baby now . . ."

MICAH, TESS, SISTERS
(Tess and Sisters join in singing and moving)
"Bye the way, Oh bye the way, When we see the preacher, we'll
say Yes sir, that's my baby . . . "

When they stop, they're all smiling.

MICAH
(shakes his head)
My ukulele progeny. Well, back to work, said Fred
(changes voices)
Back to work, said Ted.

He picks up the carton

AVA & BEEZIE
No! One more, Dad? Please!

MICAH
Really?
(looks at Tess)
Can't let down my fan base.

He strums. The other three are happy watching him play.

MICAH

(sings)

"I love to linger in the moonlight
On Honolulu Bay
My memories cling to me by moonlight
Although I'm far away"

The women join in gesturing and singing one line at a time.

TESS, MICAH, SISTERS

"If you like ukulele lady
Ukulele lady like a'you
If you like to linger where it's shady
Ukulele lady linger too

If you kiss ukulele lady
And you promise ever to be true
And she sees another ukulele
Lady foolin' 'round with you

Maybe she'll cry (an awful lot)
Maybe she'll sigh (and maybe not)
Maybe she'll find somebody else
Bye and bye—

To sing to when it's cool and shady
When it's all wicky wacky woo
If you like ukulele lady
Ukulele lady like a'you . . . "

Micah stops singing first—gradually they all stop, smiles fade as if they've all heard an absent voice . . . A silence. The sisters jump up, emotional.

BEEZIE

Okay. Gotta go!

AVA
(blurts it out)

He's too far away!

A pause

TESS

He'll always be too far away.

BEEZIE

That's not what she means, Mom.

TESS

I know what she means.

AVA
(a plea)

Closer, at least closer.

BEEZIE

Really. It would be easier for all of us.

MICAH

But it might not be better for him, uprooted.

TESS

It's where he wanted to be, remember? The sun, the surf. His choice.

AVA

He'd see us. We'd see him.

TESS

You know what it took to set everything up for him out there? Should we go over it again?

BEEZIE

We know how hard you—

MICAH

Okay, so when you guys are ready to relocate Arky, do it. We'll support you.

BEEZIE

Dad, come on.

MICAH
(heated)

What? Don't you think we've considered it? Moving a man with paranoid schizophrenia six thousand miles to a different state, different regulations.

AVA
(hands in the air)

No. Okay—let's just—

TESS

He's legally a man, not a boy anymore. Not a child.

AVA

I don't need this now.

MICAH
(trying to stay calm)

Just listen: transport security, a case manager, twenty-four seven supervised affordable housing, legal guardian, prescribing psychiatrist, psychologist, dentist, internist—insurance.

BEEZIE

But he's so fucking lonely—and miserable!

TESS

Yes. He is. And it's a knife-in-the-heart god-awful disease that doesn't improve by location. But it's the hand he's been dealt.

AVA

Okay, gotta go!

TESS

We've all been dealt.

BEEZIE

Okay, love you! Bye.

AVA

Bye, love you!

Quick hugs with their parents and they rush off. Micah and Tess watch them leave.

Micah and Tess get ready for bed, totally exhausted.

                          TESS
They took one doll each, and the ukulele.

                         MICAH
                  (removes his shoes)
Well, no hysteria, minimum of tears, and just a tad of blame. That's what I call a successful visit.

                          TESS
                      (a beat)
I saw Colleen at the gas station—his first girlfriend. Two kids in car seats. I was stunned. She has two kids! She waved.
                  (shakes her head)
I couldn't breathe.

                         MICAH
We haven't sung like that in ages.

                          TESS
Remember Colleen? Life has gone on for his girlfriends, for all his friends. Of course it has! On with their lives.

                         MICAH
                       (nods)
Beautiful girl.

> *(pause)*

Twelve years. Twelve years since we all sang together. All five of us.

> TESS
> *(fear spasm)*

Who's going to care for him, Micah? Who's going to love him when we're gone??

> MICAH
> *(comforts her)*

The girls will always love him, Tess. You know that.

> *A silence.*

> TESS

I'll never fall asleep.

> MICAH

Deep breathe. Exhale slowly.

> TESS

Where's the potato vodka?

> MICAH
> *(thinks)*

Packed.

> *A pause.*

MICAH & TESS
(simultaneously)
Did you cancel the newspaper?

> *They start to settle down. After a moment, anxiety over-takes Tess.*

TESS
We'll never make it! The house closing, the movers, the co-op closing. We don't have enough time!

MICAH
It's okay. We'll make it.

TESS
There's too much to do. Contact gas and electric, shut off here, turn on there. Confirm the movers. Get the posters to the framing shop. Remember the dump is closed Wednesdays, closed Wednesdays. And broadband! We need to switch carriers. Area rugs to the cleaners, big rugs cleaned before they're moved—maybe we should forget the big rugs. They're old. Fuck the big rugs we'll give them away. The mail! We have to forward the mail, change the magazine addresses. Send access cards to the old cable company or they'll charge us. Keys! The keys need to be copied. Micah where are the—

> *He reaches, gently pulls her down beside him.   The LIGHTS SHIFT.*

END ACT TWO

ACT THREE

Micah and Tess are still in bed.

The sisters address the audience.

AVA

Deep night and the house groans with change
Emptying, creaking sounds of change
Dad and Mom are near the end of what happened here

BEEZIE

Twelve years of slow-motion shattering
On the family Richter scale
No smoke, no fire (it couldn't be seen from outside)
And no closure

AVA

In her dreams
Mom pacing through rooms
Reciting her lists over and over and over

BEEZIE

While Dad—Dad is in turmoil
Something boiling up, surfacing and
Dad is in turmoil

MICAH
(groggy)
Tess, someone—someone's here, downstairs. I hear someone.

TESS

Wake up, Micah.

MICAH
(groggy)

He's here, downstairs.

TESS
(sharply)

You're dreaming. Wake up.

He awakens.

TESS

It's okay, sweetheart, you were dreaming.

MICAH
(long pause)

I can't leave.
(a realization overtakes him)
I can't leave him here.

TESS
(worried)

What—what is it?

MICAH
(gradual build)

His childhood. It's in this house, the yard, the driveway.

(pauses)

He laughed here. His body grew, he got strong, funny, he got handsome here. The bones of his childhood are in this house. I walk in—he surrounds me. Kitchen table, breakfast—you're all asleep upstairs, it's raining. He's five, navy blue pajamas sitting across from me asking does god wear a raincoat, asking what do you do on the honeymoon, do you mate? Lying in bed with him teaching him to read, trading sentences back and forth then whole paragraphs. Eight years old grinning as puts on his black chaps, his black cowboy hat on his birthday, saying I'm a deth-perado! Seeing him through the window gallop, high-stepping to the garage slapping his hip as if he was riding a horse. Nine years old in the driveway throwing him endless ground balls for Little League try-outs. His whole world was right here. I can feel his shoulder in my hand—his shoulder when we walked to the mail-box. His boyhood—I can't leave that here! I walk to the mailbox I can feel his shoulder in my hand now.

TESS

Micah, wherever we go he's with us.

MICAH

No! His childhood is here, here, rooted here, rooted! When I get to the front door I sense him—the visuals, smells, the boy—his presence. When I walk inside. I can't be somewhere else and feel that.

TESS

That's why we have to leave.

MICAH
(looks at her, shakes his head)
Then I lose him, his childhood, if I can't be here with it. It'll evap-orate—piss away into memories, stupid sad stupid mem-ories—into fucking stories—anecdotes!

TESS
Micah, we will crumble here, this place will fall apart around us if we don't get out now. Old and pathetic.

MICAH
(quietly)
I'll freeze. I'll freeze somewhere else.

TESS
(an arm around him)
No! I won't let you. We warm each other. We find a way. We're healthy—that's why we have to leave.
(joylessly)
We're never without him. We visit. We call. Never without him. Ever.

There is a pounding on the front door! Tess and Micah look at one another.

TESS
The movers?

MICAH
(jumping up)
The movers!

MOVER A
(calls out to truck)
Bring wardrobes!
(to Mover B)
Where's the bubblewrap?

MOVER B
(calls to truck)
Picture crates!

MOVER A
We need more tape.

MOVER B
Bubblewrap's coming.

TESS
(to Micah, energized)
I'll drive over and meet them at the co-op. You supervise here.

MICAH
(feigns anxiety)
I'm in charge?

TESS
(amused)
You the man.
(kisses him)
My sweet, beautiful man. We'll get through this, we'll change it up. We'll change it all up.

As the movers rush by, Tess is exiting.

TESS

Please don't move the piano!

MOVER A

Wow, my favorite job-related sentence.

MICAH

It's old and banged up. She's donating it.

MOVER B
(up ramp)

Lady with a heart of gold.

MOVER A

I love your wife!

MICAH

Me too.

MOVER A

Wow, that's nice. Most guys by the time we show up they want to strangle their wives.

MOVER B
(returning)

Moving can be seriously stressful.

MOVER A
(proudly, leaving)
Hey, we're number three: death in the family, divorce, moving.

MICAH
The way you load up the van, there must be a system, right?

MOVER B
Weight and size. We stack from the heaviest to the lightest, back to front.

MICAH
I guess that makes sense.

MOVER B
(shrugs, leaves)
Hey, somebody figured it out.

MOVER A
(returning)
Yeah, scientifically.

MICAH
The science of moving.

MOVER A
(leaving)
Hey, it's just back-breaking shit. Period.

MOVER B
(arriving)

With a two-year burn-out.

(to Micah)

Chief, who packed all this stuff? You did?

MICAH

I think I tore my rotator-cuff.

MOVER B
(leaving)

You shouldna done it. It's excessive.

MOVER A
(arriving, agrees)

We pack it, we move it. Everything.

MICAH

I wish I had known that.

MOVER A
(leaving)

Always read your contract.

MOVER B
(arriving)

This is a nice old house. How come you're moving?

MICAH
(finally)

Well—I guess it's time.

MOVER B

I'd like to have a house to move out of.

MOVER A
(arriving)

Oh really? And a wife? And kids? And a mortgage?

MOVER B
(leaving)

Okay, I'll give it more thought.

MICAH
(amused)

Hey, it doesn't happen all at once. It surprises you—it's—it's constantly surprising.

Tess is busy as mover B arrives.

TESS
(displeased)

The charcoal grill? Did my husband ask you to bring that here?

MOVER B

He did, yeah.

TESS

I wanted him to get rid of it.

MOVER B
(shakes his head)

Lady, you can't separate a man from his grill.

The sisters are together.

AVA

Did they close on the house yet?

BEEZIE

Tomorrow.

AVA

I'm feeling seriously strange.
(pause)
So do people think we're—weirdos, too?

BEEZIE

No. Maybe. Only stupid people.

AVA

But we're too old for it to happen to us. I mean we're way past the age.

BEEZIE

Probably.
(pause)
Let's make reservations, go visit Arky together. Just us, without Mom and Dad.

AVA

What? I'm not ready for that. I mean I will be.

BEEZIE

It's going to be on us soon.

                         AVA
I know that.

                        BEEZIE
The two of us.

                         AVA
I know!

                        BEEZIE
He'll be all ours.

                         AVA
Would you lighten up?

                        BEEZIE
Sorry.

        A beat.

                         AVA
                    (hesitates)
Okay, so I'm not really a responsible person.
               (her sister looks at her)
I realize that's what you all think. But you're wrong.

                        BEEZIE
Good. That's good to hear.

                         AVA
It totally depends on what the responsibility is.

A silence.

                          BEEZIE
We've got to stay positive. That's how we deal. Going forward
with Mom and Dad? A positive attitude.

                           AVA
Stay positive. Okay. I'll try that. I can try that.

          Back at the house, Tess and Micah step inside, look around,
          take it in.

                          TESS
Empty. We did it.

                         MICAH
Amazing. Empty. How in the world did we do that?

                          TESS
I have no memory. It was all like a—psychotic event.

                         MICAH
It's a beautiful house.

                          TESS
                         (nods)
Like the day we walked in.
                    (shakes her head)
And they're going to rip it up, change everything.

MICAH

Not for us. It'll never change for us. It's here, forever.
                    (taps his temple)
Unchangeable.

TESS

And we'll never set foot inside again.

MICAH

In dreams.

TESS

In our dreams!
                    (looking into the house)
Do you have any regrets, Micah? Marrying me, having a family?
Do you regret it?

MICAH

I'd marry you tomorrow. Marry you and live every good day and
every single dagger-to-the-heart day of it. And every kiss, every
night in bed with you. All over again. No regrets! All over again.

TESS
                    (pause)
What about my snoring?

MICAH

I could do without the snoring.

        They turn away. Micah turns back, blows a kiss into the
        house.

At the round table, they join the lawyers.

Papers start moving extra fast.

LAWYER
(passing papers to Micah and Tess)

We sign.

(to lawyer 2)

You sign.

LAWYER 2

You sign.

(passing paper)

I sign.

LAWYER
(taking paper, passing to Mica and Tess)

We sign.

(giving paper to lawyer 2)

You sign.

LAWYER 2

You sign. I sign.

LAWYER

We sign. You sign.

LAWYER 2

I sign. You sign.

                            LAWYER
                    (reaching to lawyer 2)
Your check.

                            LAWYER 2
                    (dangling check behind him)
Their check.

                            LAWYER
Your check.
                        (points behind)
Their check.

                            LAWYER 2
Our check.

                            LAWYER
                    (holds hand out to Micah)
Our keys.

        Micah with a look to Tess, hands him keys. He passes them
        to lawyer 2.

                            LAWYER 2
                    (passes key set to lawyer)
Your keys.

        The lawyer gives them to Tess. Micah smiles at her as she
        receives them.

LAWYER 2
(rises)
Congratulations to all parties. Gotta go.

LAWYER
Well!
(to Tess)
You managed all those details. And your anger.
(She nods)
Potato vodka or no potato vodka?

TESS
(shakes her head)
It got packed.

LAWYER
Admirable, admirable work.
(to Micah)
And you got out. You survived.

MICAH
I did.

LAWYER
(to Tess)
Ended with a dream, his coming out of a dream?

TESS
Exactly.

LAWYER

It can take time, but things do bubble up.

TESS

You have mysterious knowledge.

LAWYER
(shrugs, little smile)

I do a lot of closings.

The lawyer rises, bows ceremoniously to them both, returns to the bench.

Micah and Tess are alone in their new co-op.

MICAH
(gapes)

Jeezus, look at all this. I thought we got rid of so much.

TESS
(undaunted)

We did.

MICAH

Tess, there's not going to be enough space here—the clothes, furniture, books, pictures.

TESS

There's room.

MICAH
(surprised)
How do you know that?

TESS
(focused)
Stackable storage cubes, shelf dividers, partitions, expandable
shoe-cubbies, vanity shelving, overhead closet racks, under-bed
containers. It's a problem with a structural solution.

MICAH
When did you research all this?

TESS
There are world-class social engineers out there, with their fingers in the domestic socket.

MICAH
So—you've ordered those things already?

TESS
(nods)
I have tapped into organizational genius.

He smiles at her.

The sisters to the audience.

BEEZIE
The house holds its ground
It looks the same from the road, from the outside

A handsome old house, spruced up
But Dad and Mom avoid it now
They drive other streets
To reach their new home
They've made it comfortable
They've made it their own

                    AVA
We visit them, the days are calmer
But their sleep is still shallow, unsettled
They go other places in their dreams
Or to the same place
And cry out in their sleep

        They exit.

        The watercolor of the house is projected on the screen.

        At the co-op, Micah and Tess are unpacking.

                    MICAH
You know for an ex-gardener, you kept a lot of gardening books.

                    TESS
                (points)
There's a patch, that six-by-six-foot patch catches great sunlight.

                    MICAH
So—it's calling you?

                        TESS
I might be forced to dabble.

                        MICAH
Cook books in the kitchen?

                        TESS
                (looks around, shakes her head)
There's no space.

        Beezie appears down a ramp carrying clothes.

                        BEEZIE
There's room on the bottom shelf in our bookcase. Where do
these gloves and scarves go?

                        TESS
In the loft for now. Is your bus at six or seven?

                        BEEZIE
Seven.
                    (rummaging)
Dad, I thought you tossed grandma's watercolors.

                        TESS
He did toss them.

                        MICAH
Yes I did. Except for those two.

> BEEZIE
> *(laughs)*

Three.

Micah looks around behind him, fast, does it again.

> BEEZIE

What are you doing, Dad?

> MICAH
> *(low, suspicious)*

I think these boxes are reproducing behind my back.

Ava arrives with a pizza.

> AVA

One large pie, half goat cheese, half arugula and sun-dried toma-toes.
> *(looks around)*

Are there more boxes?

> BEEZIE

Mom, let's set the table outside.

> TESS

Napkins are on top of the fridge.

> AVA
> *(considering)*

You know, two really colorful area rugs would help, big time.

BEEZIE

I'm kinda getting used to all the white tiles—it's like—I don't know what it's like.

As Micah and the sisters work behind her, Tess steps down-stage.

TESS
(to the audience)

When we moved into our old house I was almost thirty. We had one beautiful baby and I was seven months pregnant. It was the most exciting time to be alive! Ten years later my three kids were a wonderful handful—all smart, funny, gorgeous, difficult. We worried about the things parents of young children are supposed to worry about: their health, accidents, evil in the world. Then, ten years after the first ten—I guess I let my guard down. How could I imagine my witty, lovable eighteen-year-old boy would lose his mind, that his mind would break and be—unfixable? But it happened. It happened and I'll never get past it. It doesn't end, while he and I breathe. I keep loving someone who is still there, but a husk now. The exterior is familiar. And I know the heart is still good.

(pause)

Everybody has trouble in life. And every day is a character test. So on we go, we "survive." Is that courage? Or just instinct? A cocktail: courage and instinct on the rocks. Make it a double.

(upbeat)

Well, we've left the house. I moved my life into a much brighter place with the man I love. We'll take walks with our sweet dog, long autumn walks, winter walks, listen for spring, hug our girls

when they visit, watch baseball, swim in the surf, and do what needs to be done. How we do it, is who we are.
>   *(smiles)*
Remember what Evel Knievel said? "Nobody's getting out of this alive."

>   AVA
Mom, where are the paper plates?

>   *Tess points her to them.*

>   MICAH
>   *(looks up)*
Tess, are you calling or am I?

>   *Before she can respond . . .*

>   AVA
>   *(surprising herself)*
I'll call. I mean—we'll both call.

>   BEEZIE
Right. We'll call him today.

>   *With a glance out at the audience, Tess nods, turns and moves upstage towards her girls and her husband.*

>   *The watercolor of the house fades. Projected onto the screen is a photo of a small clearing reaching to deep woods. In the clearing one tree, cherry, blooms.*

LIGHTS down and out.

THE END

ARKY

A Play in Three Scenes

Scene One

CONVERTIBLE

LIGHTS slam up on the lip of the stage as ARKY, a young man in blue board shorts, a gray tank top and sock-less red sneakers comes hurtling from stage right, does an off-balance tumble/somersault across the stage, stumbles, staggers and crumples. Tires screech . . . Struggling to his knees, he looks around wildly, crawls to a curb downstage left, sits slumped, dazed, breathing fast.

As LIGHTS fade down, Arky remains visible on the curb. He lifts his head slowly, stares straight out, lowers his head.

Upstage of Arky, LIGHTS rise on an attractive Airbnb apartment highlighted by a bar far upstage with comically large bottles of booze and huge plastic tumblers.

The front door down left flies open and TESS, around fifty, disheveled in shorts and a short-sleeve shirt, enters in a slow-motion, hand-over-mouth rush for the bathroom door upstage left, and disappears.

Behind her comes MICAH, mid-fifties on all-fours, wearing shorts, a NY Mets baseball cap and a vest. He crawls in exhausted slow motion to the bar, pulls himself up, breathing hard, hesitates, then with two hands pours a drink into one of the oversized glasses.

*He looks at it, puts it right down, and as Tess exits the bath-
room Micah rushes for it in real time. Tess moves to the
bar, sees his drink, lifts it with both hands and takes a
healthy slug. She exhales. Micah steps from the bathroom,
wasted. He joins Tess at the bar. She hands him the tumb-
ler, pours a drink for herself.*

                          MICAH
                    (raises his tumbler)
Bon appetit.

                           TESS
                    (lifts her tumbler)
Auf wiedersehen.

       They smile wanly at one another, gulp whiskey.

                          MICAH
                       (exhales)
Holy shite.

                           TESS
                    (simultaneously)
Good god.

         They drink again, catch their breath.

                          MICAH
I left the car thing in the car. What do you call it now? Not keys.

                              TESS

Electronic—key-replacement—object.

                              MICAH
                             (nods)

Thing.

              A pause.

                              TESS

He'll sleep. They've got him all drugged up.
                            (pause)
You didn't say anything before, did you, anything negative—to
set him off? It doesn't take much.

                              MICAH

"Good morning, Arky."

                              TESS

He wouldn't say a word to me. Just climbed in back, over the
door—folded his arms and sat there, wouldn't look at me.

                              MICAH

Then I asked where he wanted to go for coffee.
                            (shrugs)
Nothing. So I said Cafe YaYa, fifteen minutes across the bridge
we'll get our espresso.
                            (pause)
Whatever was going on he brought with him. He was angry.
Maybe he didn't take his meds. I bet he hasn't been taking his
meds.

TESS
(regretfully)
Cafe YaYa—my coconut muffin sold to a stranger.

She turns to him and they embrace, a long, tender moment.

TESS
Well, I've got pills for us—to sleep.

MICAH
(picks up his drink)
You read about this, it doesn't happen to you.

TESS
Maybe we're in shock. Is shock physiological or psychological?

She pulls out her phone, looking for information.

MICAH
That guy who came over to help was a doctor—in his bathing suit.
When I told him, he said his brother had schizophrenia. Orange
and white bathing suit.

TESS
(looking at cellphone)
"In shock."

MICAH

I wanted to hug the guy—getting out of his car on a bridge—just somebody—for coming over—for his dopey creamsicle bathing suit—for understanding. What are you doing?

TESS
(focused on phone)
It's one of those terms we think we know.

MICAH

You realize we almost had a fight, an argument right there.

TESS

When?

MICAH

Right there when we got out of the car! Who should call 911, who should go over to him. You started to argue with me.

TESS
(looks up, sharply)
But I called, didn't I? I wanted to run to my son but I didn't do it. I called 911 instead because you said so.
(pause)
What took you so long—to stop? (she looks at him) To pull over and stop.

MICAH
(troubled)
What? I—I'm not sure.

TESS

Just to stop. What took you so goddam long?

MICAH
(hesitates)

I didn't see him—jump—I was driving.

TESS

He didn't "jump."

MICAH

What?

TESS

I yelled at you to pull over and you questioned me, you said: Why? And I shouted: he left! He left the car!
(shakes her head)
Then you started to scream—but you kept going, kept driving. And you kept screaming.

MICAH

Scream—Was I scream—
(realizes)
I was. I was screaming the whole time—from the moment you told me. Jeezus I can hear myself. I can hear me screaming like— like a—I wasn't aware of it.
(pauses)
There were cars behind me—I was screaming—on the bridge, forty miles an hour. I couldn't just stop, slam on the—I wanted to pull over. I wanted to, I—I couldn't do it. It didn't register—it took a hundred fucking yards.

(a beat)
You're right, maybe I was in shock.

TESS
(points to cellphone)
Nope. It's from your body—caused by bodily trauma—a reaction. "A psychological reaction to bodily trauma." We are not, by definition, in shock. What we are is really really fucked up,

MICAH
Unconscious screaming is what? Terrified animal response, right?

TESS
The corner of my eye—I turned.

MICAH
Death terror. Like a rabbit under an owl.

TESS
He was on his feet stepping onto the door frame. So I did what any terrified animal would do. Screamed "Micah."

TESS
I opened my mouth nothing came out. Then he—went over—he left. Just stepped out. Like he was going for a walk.

MICAH
(shakes his head)
And kept screaming.

He drinks.

                          TESS

It was so—casual. Something almost—Buster Keaton silly, stepping out of a moving car—ridiculous.

She drinks.

                          MICAH

Just a pathetic reaction. Outside my comprehension. No prior experience with—with moving vehicle departures.

                          TESS

Then I'm on the phone with some 911 moron trying to be co-her-
ent watching you move towards Arky, watching him hunched
over on the curb, people staring from their cars—like we're on
display: "See the Frantic Parents . . ."

                          MICAH

I tried to run to him but—

                          TESS

". . . a Living Diorama!"

                          MICAH

I couldn't do it. It was like running in wet cement, wet cement up
to my waist. The harder I tried to move my legs the slower I went.
I could see him bent over on the curb and I couldn't reach him! I
could hardly breathe! The adrenalin—I was exhausted in seconds—slogging getting nowhere—finally I just—I walked! It was

comical. My kid jumps out of a moving car and I'm fucking walk-ing, I'm walking to him! Cars all stopped, people gawking at him and I'm strolling—"just out for stroll folks—that's my son over there!" I even thought about getting down, all fours—craw-ling to him. It crossed my mind, it did—maybe I can reach him faster if I—scurry. But I didn't. I saw myself—I didn't like the image. So I just kept—trudging along! It took me—it felt like hours!

(pause)

Whose kid jumps out of a moving car on a bridge?? Well, mine. My kid. Ours. Our kid. Oh god—our life!

TESS

He didn't jump!

(shoots him a look)

I told you.

He drinks, turns downstage.

TESS

Maybe we should pack. Or I could shower—and wash it off. Wash it all off! We've got to do a laundry. Micah? Right now I'm—I feel really—

(shrugs)

Strange.

LIGHTS SHIFT to Arky sitting on the curb as Micah steps towards him.

MICAH
(breathing very hard)
Arky I'm here! Dad's here. It's okay, going to be okay. You're sitting up, that's good! Good. Just don't move honey, please don't
move.
(sits beside him, looks him over, winces seeing blood but doesn't
touch him)
I'm right here. We called. Mom called 911, there's an ambulance
coming. I'm right here. I love you Arky. Please just stay still.
(Arky hasn't moved or looked at him)
We'll stay right here with you. Are you hurting? You must be hurting somewhere—it's—it's a beautiful day and—people are coming to help us. We love you, Arky. We aren't leaving.

As LIGHTS SHIFT back into the suite, Arky remains on the
curb. Micah has pulled out a small pad and is taking notes,
as Tess comes out of the bathroom her hair in a towel,
drinking. (NOTE: Micah writes on the pad throughout.)

TESS
What about that woman, the long red skirt? She was in the car
right behind us.

MICAH
(looks up from his pad)
She handed him her business card.

TESS
I was glad she came over, whoever she was.

MICAH

Offering "psychic assistance."

TESS

She kept patting his knee and calling him sweetheart.

MICAH
(taking notes)

The more psychic assistance she gave him the more she sounded like a complete herbal nut-job.

TESS
(drinks, sudden worry)

Did we thank her? Before they all arrived? People who are kind to him, whoever they are, must be thanked. Kind people must be thanked no matter what.

MICAH

All those sirens, the EMTs, fire trucks, police cars.

TESS

I can't remember—did you thank her? Did you??

He looks up from his notes, nods.

TESS

Oh good. That's good.

MICAH

Finally, the goddam ambulance. I'm on the curb with him, hearing the sirens and you know what I flash on? His fireman's hat, and

the cowboy outfit—boots, spurs, black hat and that vest, the little
light bulbs that went on and off.

TESS
(smiles)
He went to bed in that vest. I couldn't get it off him—watching
the lights blink till he fell asleep. And I'd go back in and turn off
the vest. Sneak another kiss and—inhale him.

A pause. They drink.

MICAH
Forty miles an hour and just a few stitches, staples in his scalp.
Amazing.

TESS
He should be dead. I mean the EMTs and that porky cop sort of
implied it, right? Everyone was so nice. But I kept wondering
what are they really thinking? "The guy gets up and just steps out
of a moving vehicle? What did they do? What did they say to him?
What kind of people are they?"

MICAH
I can't tell if I'm hungry or not.

He goes to the fridge.

TESS
Why do I care about their opinions?

MICAH
(looking into fridge)
What goes with alcohol?

TESS
Or anybody's goddam opinion—as if they had a clue what it's like! What it's been like.

MICAH
Something semi-healthy.

TESS
(a realization)
Maybe he was told to leave the car.

He looks up at her.

TESS
His voices. A command. Something he had to do.

MICAH
"Hey Arky, let's get away from these two assholes."

TESS
If he's been off his meds—I bet.
(nods, drinks)
How can you think about food?

MICAH
My voices tell me I haven't eaten since breakfast.

TESS

I just want to drink.

Micah carries a wedge of cheese to the bar.

MICAH
(refills his drink)

Well, I'm good at both. Food and drink. That's what two hands are for. If I only had one hand I'd probably be an alcoholic.
(considers)
Maybe I am an alcoholic.

TESS
(drinks)

Go for it.

MICAH

I would bet you're an alcoholic.

TESS

You would? Who cares? We left the planet years ago. We're out there—just out there in orbit, visiting our boy in Crazyland.

MICAH

The girls care.

TESS
(a regal wave)

All our friends waving to us from Normal-land.
(sharply)
We do not tell the girls about today.

MICAH

They should know what's happening here in Crazyland with their brother.

TESS

Down the road. They don't need details right now. It'll be less scary put in the past, like—like history.

She drinks.

MICAH

"By the way, girls, the reason we don't rent convertibles any more..."

TESS
(rueful)
They'll get their chance for vivid details once they're in charge— their "inheritance."

A pause. They drink.

MICAH

Something happens to you—truly dreadful—everything else just—the rest of the world, all the awful stuff—starvation, mass-acres, rapes, beheadings—it gets—distanced, you can't hold onto the "big picture," suicide bombers, drowning refugees—you can't carry them with you because you're all filled up with your own personal-pain-shit. There's no room left in the backpack.

TESS

What makes you think I'm an alcoholic?

MICAH

You drink all the time.

(pauses)

And I drink most of the time.

(with a laugh)

We're miserable!

TESS

(grins)

I'll drink to that.

(raises her glass with two hands)

Gesundheit!

MICAH

(raises his glass with two hands)

Viva Zapata!

They drink.

MICAH

So, are we packing? Out by noon tomorrow?

TESS

(drinks)

We'd all be better off if he'd cracked himself open dead on the bridge.

(looks at Micah)

Wouldn't we? Wouldn't he? What kind of life is he going to have??

(pause)

Don't you think? Better off?

MICAH

Well, he teaches hard lessons, cosmic lesson.

TESS

Please. I don't need any more "hard lessons."

MICAH
(drinks)
Maybe it transcends our needs.

TESS
(stung)
Oh? What is it about then? Wait—wait, could this all be more val-
uable "material"? Is that what—raw material—your "notes"—get
it all down on paper, write something new, really clever and pow-
erful? These "hard lessons," more research?

MICAH

Yes. I refuse to let things just happen—accepted, un-examined.
How's that?

TESS

And does it make you feel good, using his—misfortune, his illness
for your work? Or—shabby? Feeling kind of shabby?

        He drinks.

MICAH

It's how I try to make sense of it. What I do.

TESS

Ah, I see. Of course. Analytical.

MICAH

And what do you do? You obsess. You talk. You talk obsessively. Talk talk talk talk to your fascinated friends—talk talk talk. And drink. That's what you do to make sense of it, of why someone nineteen goes bonkers. And we both fail—to make any sense of it, of him. We fail because making sense of insanity is absurd! It's pointless. But we keep trying—years, because he's ours! Our nut-job. Our boy—our thirty-year-old boy.

He turns for the bedroom stage left with his drink.

The LIGHTS SHIFT as Tess moves downstage talking to Arky on the curb. She sits beside him. He doesn't move or look at her.

TESS

Dad's with the EMTs. They're going to put you on a gurney, strap you down in case there's a problem with your neck, or your back. They won't let me sit in the ambulance with you but we'll be right behind in the car. We'll follow you straight to the hospital.
                    (pause)
I love you Arky! I'm so sorry.
                    (looking up she sees the gurney approaching)
The gurney—just—listen to instructions. They seem very kind. I'm sorry this happened, this—accident. I don't want you ever to be hurt!
                    (tentatively touches his arm, he doesn't move)
My son, my shining boy.

                    (rises, beckons the EMTs)
We love you, Arky. Just follow directions. They understand—who
you are.

> *Arky remains on the curb. LIGHTS SHIFT back to the suite
> as Tess moves into it and Micah comes out of the bathroom
> with a laundry basket.*

                          TESS
Let's stay.

> *He looks at her.*

                          TESS
I know, I know—change flights, find another place—but just a
few more days. We can't leave him now, Micah.

                          MICAH
He won't remember if we stayed three minutes or three days.
He's in good hands.

                          TESS
Not after something like this.

                          MICAH
He'll be observed, they won't just release him. We'll visit in the
morning before the plane. He chose to live here—he insisted.

                          TESS
He's hurt.

MICAH

Abrasions. Stitches and staples. Not one broken bone, you heard the doctor.

TESS

He's in the hospital. He needs his parents.

He drinks.

MICAH

He just made a serious attempt to escape his parents.
(a pause)
He'll be taken home, medicated, visited. This is about you, not Arky.

TESS

What if it is? I'm the mother.

MICAH

People say two words: child, hospital. That means you're supposed to be there. It's expected—doing the right—the acceptable right thing.

TESS

Don't generalize me, Micah. "People say." Don't you dare generalize me.

MICAH

Packing, unpacking, cancelling flights, booking flights, finding a place, switching places, going back and forth to another goddam hospital.

TESS
(little smile, drinks)
You just hate to spend the money.

MICAH
Right.

TESS
(grins, points at him)
Tight with a dollar!

MICAH
I hate to spend the money.

TESS
Even with his son in the hospital.
(laughs)
He's tight with a dollar!

She goes to the bar.

MICAH
Okay! We've got to get away from here. This is—guess what—this is harder on us than on him. He's drugged up, no pain. We are a collective fucking disaster.

TESS
(pouring more booze)
I have no idea what you're burbling about.

MICAH

Just tell me before you totally obliterate yourself, do you need to stay? Or is it a "should," that you feel you should stay? Come on dig deep: need or should? Because if you really need to stay, a visceral fucking need, I'll go on line for a new place, extend the car rental and cancel the goddam flight.

A pause.

TESS

(flat, not looking at him)

I want to run away. From everybody who knows me: "the mother loser." Disappear. Dig a hole to China, climb in, cover myself with wet dirt and—roar. Roar. Primal—primal until the blood vessels pop in my throat, my neck, in my head—explode me!

(pause)

That's what I "need." The "should" part is everything above ground. Does that answer your stupid question?

MICAH

(gently)

Nobody thinks of you that way.

TESS

No! I don't want to hear it—immaterial. Allow me the pleasure of wallowing in self-disgust. It's one of the few pleasures I have left.

MICAH

We can stay a couple more days. It's not that big a deal.

A pause.

TESS

Another thousand dollars.

MICAH

About. Maybe more. Probably more. More.

TESS
(considers)
Then—no. I vote no. I'm a cheapskate—we're a couple.

She drinks.

MICAH

We've got the money.

TESS

Nope. But I want to see how he is in the morning. And what the doctor says. And that nurse. The one you were looking at—with the tits. She seemed smart.

MICAH

Actually, I was looking at the one with the legs, who seemed stupid. You should know that by now. But we don't need anybody else's opinion to tell us about staying or going.

TESS

That is not—these are my feelings, my feelings! My son just walked out of a car at forty miles an hour.

MICAH
(low)

Jumped. He jumped out of a fucking convertible.

With a feral, guttural, drunken growl Tess leaps at him, arms swinging, punching out. Micah tries to fend her off but she's wild, pounding on him.

MICAH

Stop! Goddamit Tess.

He backs away, arms raised in defense as she keeps flailing.

MICAH

Stop, stop it!

Hysterical, she continues swinging at him. He manages to move in, gets past her arms, grabs her, pulls her close. She keeps pounding his back, his shoulders. He lifts her off the ground—buries his head in the side of her neck and suddenly they are passionately going at each other—yanking at clothes—he tugs at her shorts, she pulls at his vest. They're locked in, drunkenly tearing at one another.

LIGHTS dip slowly as they grapple, sinking to their knees.

A pool of WHITE LIGHT drops onto Arky, who slowly rises. There's blood down his neck, on his tank top, blood all over him.

A low, sonorous electric bass chord thrums, filling the air.

In shadow, Micah and Tess slide into one another.

ARKY

(sings—a gorgeous clear voice)

Fly!
Arky fly!
Stand up and fly
Arky save the Muslims
Arky save the Jews
And shine,
Shine always
Shine everywhere
Shine like the sun
Shine like the sun
And fly
They said fly
Stand up you can fly
Arky you can fly!

BLACKOUT

Scene Two

PRODUCTS

Ten years later.

ARKY Enters a Starbucks downstage left: balding, limping slightly, aging badly. He's in an old tank top, flowery board shorts, new neon-green sneakers. He walks deliberately, a large coffee cup in hand. He's aware of other patrons, all pillow DUMMIES, sitting nearby.

ARKY
(to himself)

No more ciggies no more chew
No beer no wine Americano brew Americano brew
Lookin' for my stall lookin' for my stall
I'm walkin' Spanish walkin'
Spanish down the hall

(looks around furtively, low)

Pray for the Muslims pray for the Jews
Pray for the Muslims no booze no booze
Pray for the Jews single-malt Jews

He glances behind him, sits at a small table, sips his coffee, looks over his shoulder. He rises, does a short, oddly grace-ful dance, the sits quickly.

> ARKY
> *(glancing around)*

'Scuse me, 'Scuse me.

> *LIGHTS dip but stay low on Arky at his table with a coffee and a newspaper.*

> *LIGHTS up on the suggestion of an upscale hotel suite. In the middle stands BEEZIE, mid-thirties, in high platform wedges, stylish jeans, and a T-shirt.*

> *She's lugging a serviceable piece of roller luggage and a shoulder bag. She drops the shoulder bag on a chair.*

> BEEZIE
> *(calls off)*

It's great, Ava! Really nice. Come on.

> AVA'S VOICE

How nice?

> BEEZIE

Really, I like it.

> AVA'S VOICE

Clean? Seriously clean?

> BEEZIE
> *(amused)*

Looks clean to me.

AVA'S VOICE

Just check. Please?

Beezie swings around the suite, opens the bedroom door upstage left, disappears into it, comes out, heads into a bathroom downstage of the bedroom.

Stealthily, cautiously, as if something might snap at her, AVA, the older sister by three years, Enters in dark glasses and a long black designer coat, platform wedges like Beezie's. Her streaked blonde hair is flowing with attention. Her roller luggage, comic-book large, coordinates with her shoulder bag. She removes her sunglasses and takes the place in, not delighted.

BEEZIE'S VOICE

All clear!
                            (steps into view)
Nothing alive, nothing—moving.
                            (sees her sister)
No foreign hairs.

Ava shoots her a look.

BEEZIE

I swear! No hair anywhere. I did not see one strange hair, not at the sinks, not at the toilet, or in the shower, or on the bedspreads.

Ava starts to speak.

BEEZIE

Or the pillows! I think you can exhale.

AVA

Please don't make fun of me.

BEEZIE

No. Sorry. I'm not. Really I'm not, Aav.

AVA
(accepts it)

A shower curtain or a door?

Beezie looks at her.

AVA

Plastic shower curtains are germ-central. I will not stay here if it's a curtain.

Beezie hesitates, trying to recall. She turns around, exits back to the bathroom, returns.

BEEZIE

Door.

AVA
(nods)

And—just—would you check the mattresses, please? Just raise the bedding.

Beezie stares at her.

AVA

For bedbugs. Any—squashings. It's not unusual—travelers do it.

Beezie nods, returns to the bedroom.

AVA
(calls after her)

How do you like the wedges? They're fun, right? And comfortable? After a while?

BEEZIE'S VOICE

Yeah, surprisingly. After a while.

AVA
(puts her shoulder bag on a chair)

I think it looks buzzier when we wear them together. I mean me wearing them and you in flats would look kind of off. That's why I got them.

BEEZIE
(reappears)

Right. Thanks. They're fun. No—squashings.

She sits, removes wedges, rubs her feet.

AVA
(concerned)

Did you pack slippers?

Beezie shakes her head, No.

                              AVA

What's underfoot can be nasty. We'll get you slippers. You were
Okay with business-class? I was kind of relieved.

                             BEEZIE

You kidding? I loved it.
                             (beat)
Should we go right over there, or what?

                              AVA

No. No—let's—we need an approach. This could be really
tricky—scary even. So we should unpack. I mean for wrinkles, if
we're going to stay here. I don't imagine there's a concierge. And
I need a nest—for my products and my pills.
                         (looks around)
Like a safe haven. Over there, I think. How are the closets?

                             BEEZIE

That's the kitchenette.

                              AVA

So?

                             BEEZIE

Food preparation?

                              AVA

We're not going to eat here.

                             BEEZIE

We're not? At all?

> ### AVA
> Well, snacks, I suppose, room service. How are the closets, did you check?

> ### BEEZIE
> What? Adequate—immaculate!
> *(pause)*
> Don't you keep your products and pills in the bathroom?

> ### AVA
> At home.
> *(looks around)*
> You know there's a Four Seasons under construction.

> ### BEEZIE
> Around the corner.

> ### AVA
> So why does it take forever to build a fucking hotel? People are in need.

> ### BEEZIE
> This place is nice, Aav. It's a lot nicer than where Mom and I stayed the last couple times.

> ### AVA
> Doesn't surprise me.
> *(pauses)*
> I have to be surrounded by beauty, Okay? People and objects. I admit it—I'm shallow! But that's my weakness—well, the major one. I believe in beauty, I don't believe in love. Love sucks on a

continuing basis. Beauty just gives me a kind of—some peace of mind and—I don't know—reassurance.

BEEZIE

And appearance, is that so significant, too?

AVA

Yeah? Appearance is who you choose to present—your self-value. You can't get in the door on "character." Appearance might be superficial, but it's seriously superficial. And it's not about money. All this with Arky, these years—suppose we—I can't imagine how I'd live a day just—bare—without fashion, without my products—just exposed, uncovered, everything on display—all my fucking nerve endings! What it's done to us, to Mom.

BEEZIE

She didn't care how she "appeared."

AVA

She should have! She was so exposed it was embarrassing. She always looked the way she felt. That's a mistake. Why show the world? It's none of their business. What it did to her.
(shakes her head)
You've got to constantly be on guard. She didn't fight it. She just gave in. Everything was about—him—she Arky'd herself to death.
(tears up)
I'm sorry. I think I need—maybe five milligrams of Valium. Or two and a half. I could try two and a half to go see him. I don't want to be loopy, but I can't be too scattered, you know?

(starts to wheel her gigantic suitcase to the bedroom)
Beezie, how many Ambien did you bring? If I run out.

BEEZIE
I've got enough. You won't run out.

Relieved, Ava exits into the bedroom.

BEEZIE
(loud enough for Ava to hear)
Maybe we're better off seeing him at the Starbucks. It's more neutral, you know? Every time I go there with him he never ass-ociates with anyone. He might be—I don't—in a public place more contained—restrained? If we go to The Port—the home—whatever it's called, it's unpredictable.
(shrugs)
Maybe it doesn't matter.
(pauses)
You know, you've got to start calling him, Aav. He can't just be hearing from me. He's already wondering why he hasn't heard from Mom.

AVA
(enters carrying extra-large product tubes and pill jars, her arms filled with them)
I know. I've been too stressed.
(takes them to counter)
He'd sense it in my voice. I Amazoned him a pair of sneakers.

BEEZIE

More sneakers?

AVA
(talks as she exits back to bedroom)
Maroon! He likes different colors. I do what I can! I've been feeling shitty—calling him hasn't been a priority.

BEEZIE

Well, that's got to change now. I can't do it alone.
(a pause)
He's always at the Starbucks for a couple hours, like from two to
four or five. He needs the caffeine. Then he goes back home, to
the Port. We've still got time to go.

AVA
(returns with more extra-large tubes and jars)
If he can keep a schedule like that you'd think he could do something by now. Some—work-related activity?

BEEZIE
(surprised)

A job?

AVA
(arranging the counter with her products)
Yeah.

Beezie shakes her head, No.

                    AVA

It's still a possibility, right?

                   BEEZIE

He can hardly put a sentence together.

                    AVA

There are jobs where you don't have to relate, aren't there?
Like—like, I don't know, lifting boxes, storing things?

                   BEEZIE

Well, that requires arriving on time, some focus, following directions.

                    AVA

Lifting a box?

                   BEEZIE

Carrying it someplace, stack it, return, get another one, stack it
evenly.

                    AVA

Okay! Okay, I just thought—I was hoping.

                   BEEZIE

Well, you haven't been out here to see.

                    AVA

You have to throw that at me now?

> BEEZIE

I mean the deterioration.

> AVA

I'm here now, aren't I?

> BEEZIE

And look what it took.

> AVA
> *(looks at her)*

Bitch.

> BEEZIE

Dick.

A beat, and they both laugh. Beezie starts to get teary.

> BEEZIE

We left so fast—so soon. Christ—I'm—

> AVA
> *(comes over to her)*

Well, that was the plan.

> BEEZIE

I know. I know. It wouldn't have been fair to him, waiting. It was just so—abrupt.

Ava, with a look at the chair for cleanliness, sits beside her, puts an arm around her neck.

LIGHTS dip on them, bump up on Arky in Starbucks.

ARKY

Americano brew Americano brew
 Jump-start the brain pump out the pain
Deep in the brain calm down the brain
Knead out the pain pain in the brain

*He rises, does a short dance, sits down fast. He looks
around, hearing ancient voices.*

*[NOTE: LIGHTS dip briefly when Arky hears voices/ mom-
ents from the past.]*

ARKY
(as a five-year-old with a lisp)

When are we going? When are we going? Beezie, what are you
doing?

AVA
(as a nine-year-old)

Beezie come on.

ARKY
(five-year-old)

Christmas lights, Hanukkah nights, Christmas lights, Hanukkah
nights!

AVA
(nine-year-old)

We'll be late for the animals!

                         BEEZIE
                    (as a six-year-old)
Where's Dad?

                          ARKY
                     (five-year-old)
The animals might poop in church!

                          AVA
                     (nine-year-old)
Mom's waiting. Dad's not going.

                          ARKY
                     (five-year-old)
Cause he's Jewish, right?

                         BEEZIE
                     (six-year-old)
We're Jewish, too.

                          AVA
                     (nine-year-old)
We're only half.

                          ARKY
                     (five-year-old)
Let's be whole Jewish like Dad!

                          AVA
                     (nine-year-old)
Come on, we'll miss the animals.

ARKY
(five-year-old)
Christmas lights, Hanukkah nights, Christmas lights.
(He stops, suddenly scared, looks around. As himself:)
'Scuse me, 'scuse me.

He sits back down, grabs a coffee cup.

LIGHTS dim, hold on Arky, shift back up on the sisters.

The kitchenette counter is a confusion of extra-large tubes and jars.

Beezie closes the front door to the suite.

BEEZIE
Thank you!
(carries a food tray to a table)
Cheese and crackers look terrific!

Ava comes out of the bedroom in shorts and a T-shirt carrying one last extra-large product tube.

AVA
This moisturizer is gold—French, unbelievable. Did you bring your stomach meds?

Beezie nods.

AVA
I can't shake this headache.

> BEEZIE

Hydrate. And eat.

Ava comes over and joins her at the table.

> AVA

It's stress.
> *(checks out the cheese)*

I feel like—like an octopus victim—so many things squeezing at once. Losing Mom, worrying about Arky, my own health, harvesting my eggs, or not.

> BEEZIE
> *(glances at her)*

Try the camembert.

> AVA

As soon as one lets up, another one takes its place and squeezes! Now we've got this entire goddam service at home to plan.

> BEEZIE

Maybe we should think of it as an opportunity.

Ava looks at her.

> BEEZIE

To celebrate Mom, her life?

                              AVA

I really hate soft cheese. I mean I like it but it's bad for digestion.
That's what Ryna says, for the bowels. She says if you're going to
eat cheese only eat hard cheese. The cheddar looks suspicious.

                             BEEZIE

She's your dietician?

                              AVA

She prefers health consultant.

                             BEEZIE
                             (nods)
So—you're really going to harvest your eggs, do an in-vitro?

                              AVA

I don't want to talk about it.

          Beezie shoots her a look.

                              AVA

What?

                             BEEZIE

You brought it up.

                              AVA

I referred to it. We can discuss it later. Or not.
                    (cuts a slice of cheese)
This better be fresh.

(hesitates, tries it—acceptable)
Did Mom tell you she wanted a "celebration"?

Beezie shakes her head, No.

                    AVA
We did it for Dad doesn't mean it's right for her. She was miserable. He wasn't.

                    BEEZIE
She wasn't always.

                    AVA
Don't get weepy.

                    BEEZIE
She allowed herself to be—consumed.

                    AVA
Because she wasn't invested in anything else.

                    BEEZIE
Like—she put on whatayacallit—blinders—to the whole outside world.

                    AVA
Dad at least had his notes, his projects.

                    BEEZIE
The last ten years—everything Arky, Arky twenty-four-seven.

(shakes her head)

Fucking blinders.

(pauses)

I'm—this is weird. I'm feeling—what am I feeling?

AVA

She like—retracted—from life.

BEEZIE

(surprised)

You know, I think I'm experiencing some kind of—passive aggressive—it's like an anger thing.

(little laugh)

No—I'm actually—I am. I'm angry!

AVA

Good for you. I'm going to try the gouda.

BEEZIE

She was so focused on him all the time. I kept—I crawled right
into it with her.

(shakes her head)

To stay close to her, connected—by worrying about him.

AVA

Yeah. And where did that leave me?

BEEZIE

This isn't about you. It's my revelation, all right? Me, not you, for
once.

Ava raises her hands in surrender.

> BEEZIE

Now she's gone and I'm angry—I'm angry at her! How pathetic is that?

Ava offers Beezie a cracker with cheese.

> AVA

The Gouda is totally acceptable. Try it.

> BEEZIE
> *(a threat)*

I try the Gouda, when you try the fucking Camembert.

They look at one another.

LIGHTS SHIFT to Arky at the table, a couple of large coffee cups in front of him. He's rocking back and forth in his chair.

LIGHTS dip.

> BEEZIE
> *(as a teenager)*

Arky, what's wrong?

> ARKY
> *(troubled teen)*

Sports and capitalism: survival of the fittest. You name it.

AVA
(as a teenager)

We're going for sushi.

ARKY
(troubled teen)

You name it.

BEEZIE
(teenager)

Do you want to talk about it?

ARKY
(troubled teen, looks up, smiles)

Love you. Love you both!

AVA
(teenager)

Come with, for sushi—or pizza?

ARKY
(troubled teen)

Pizza or sushi?
(shakes his head)

This buzzing—like bees buzzing, roaring around.
(looks up)

It's ridiculous.

AVA
(teen)

Please come.

                            ARKY
                        (troubled teen)
Is there a plan? You think there's a plan? I mean a master plan?

                           BEEZIE
                            (teen)
Sweetheart.

                            ARKY
                        (troubled teen)
Okay, but something is burning.

                           BEEZIE
                            (teen)
Mom's going to find someone for you to talk to—she will.

                            AVA
                            (teen)
A doctor.

                           BEEZIE
                            (teen)
Come with?

        LIGHTS bump up.

                            ARKY
            (as HIMSELF, looks around, calms himself)
Two vente mocha frappacinos
Caramel lattes side-by-side
That girl just smiled!

Dark hair blue eyes
And a Cuban cigar Cuban cigar
Cuban cigar

Two vente mocha frappacinos
 Caramel lattes side-by-side
A girl who smiles
Dark hair blue eyes
Dark hair blue eyes
And a Cuban cigar
Cuban cigar
Cuban cigar
                    (realizing he's talking aloud)
'Scuse me, 'scuse me.
Pray for the Muslims.
Pray for the Jews.
'Scuse me.

        LIGHTS shift back to the sisters, eating cheese and crackers

                    AVA
Why do I associate runny Camembert with kids—and snot.

        She eats.

                    BEEZIE
Ever wonder why we haven't achieved family? Everybody we
know has a baby.

                    AVA
A tit sucker, a toddler. I want one.

BEEZIE

Okay, I'm going to say a word and as soon as you hear it say whatever comes into your head.

Ava nods. They've played this before.

BEEZIE

Here's the word: pregnancy.

AVA

Mice.

BEEZIE

Mice??

AVA

I don't know, do I really want a child with all that—drooling? Or do I just want something I can sort of—mold, you know? That will totally adore me, need me—so I could be seriously obsessed with something other than men or products or fashion. I'm not really sure.

BEEZIE

I never thought you were interested in kids.

AVA

I wasn't. People change. It's biology. Maybe a large dog.

BEEZIE
(carefully)

You don't seem so maternal to me.

                    AVA

I can be maternal.

                    BEEZIE

Okay.

                    AVA

Part of it creeps me out though—I mean it grows inside you!
Grows, inside—and I keep seeing this—I don't see a fetus, okay?
I see a guy's dick wearing Ray-Bans and flip-flops—with little
hands paddling around, waiting to get out, get free! It's kind of a
turn-off.

        Beezie shakes her head, amused.

                    AVA

What? Men go wild for me—even after they hear about Arky—
and my two divorces. Pretty soon they figure out the percentages
for crazy kids and back off.

                    BEEZIE

They run. Guys run.

                    AVA

Maybe they start to see me as a sort of—beautiful out-patient.

                    BEEZIE

That's good.

                    AVA

Meaning what?

                           BEEZIE
                    (frustrated with her)
Nothing. It was just well-put.

                            AVA
So what happened with the Japanese guy, you never said. Kay?
That lasted a while.

                           BEEZIE
Kai.

                            AVA
He was buff.

                           BEEZIE
He's American.

                            AVA
Well, he appeared Japanese.

                           BEEZIE
                         (bothered)
Could we talk about what we're going to say to Arky, how we're
going to tell him, and get moving?

                            AVA
Kai was a little creepy.

                           BEEZIE
What?

                          AVA

I mean the way he looked at me—like you weren't even in the
room.

                         BEEZIE
                         (shrugs)

He's a psychologist.

                          AVA
                        (worried)

What did you tell him? That I was at a spa, right? That I had just
gotten back from a high-end spa?

                         BEEZIE
                         (nods)

What difference does it make now, really?

                          AVA

He only met me once. It's not enough to make a judgment, one
"session."

     Beezie shakes her head, senses where it's going.

                          AVA

One fucking drink.

                         BEEZIE
                        (gently)

There was no judgment, it wasn't a "session."

AVA

(rises)

Maybe he got tired of your good deeds.

BEEZIE

(surprised)

Why are you being mean to me?

AVA

Because—you suffocate me. I can't breathe around you!

LIGHTS SHIFT to Arky, who gets to his feet quickly.

ARKY

(angry, late teens)

I'm not having any "tests," okay?

BEEZIE

(upset, around twenty)

They're trying to help you.

ARKY

(late teens)

It's bullshit. They're both—Dad—both of them—they're—it's bullshit.

AVA

(scared, early twenties)

They're worried, Arky.

ARKY
(late teens)
Nothing is wrong, they're fucking with me.

AVA
(early twenties)
They just want to make—

ARKY
(late teens)
No tests. Not going to happen. No tests.

BEEZIE
(around twenty)
We all love you, Arky.

ARKY
(late teens, very upset)
My brain—my brain is none of their—nobody's—nobody's—it's
nobody's!

    LIGHTS bump up.

ARKY
(HIMSELF, calming himself)
Lights go down the lights go down
Dark and it all goes dark
Who do you see? Who do you see?
Strike the match
Strike the match
Me? Is that me shining?

Me in the dark?
Arky's shining Arky's shining
 Arky's shining in the dark
                    (looks around)
'Scuse me, 'scuse me.
Save the Muslims no booze no booze.
Save the Jews single-malt Jews.

         He sits at his table.

         LIGHTS SHIFT back to the sisters.

                    BEEZIE
                   (fed up)
Okay, I'm going to tell him it was sudden.

                    AVA
I need—what do I need? Valium, right. Two and a half milligrams.

                    BEEZIE
A shock to everybody and we came out right away to tell him.

                    AVA
                   (shrugs)
Five.

                    BEEZIE
Heart attack—boom.

                    AVA
That's a little crude.

BEEZIE

Oh?

AVA

We should be able to position it better than that.

BEEZIE

Position it?

AVA

Yeah! With some tact, some nuance.

BEEZIE

She's dead. That kind of puts a crimp in nuance.

AVA

Dude, I don't want to spin him out in the middle of a Starbucks, do you? We've seen that movie.

BEEZIE
(weighs it)
So breaking it to him what—gently?

AVA

Foreshadow it, maybe some foreshadowing. So it won't hit him so hard—lead up to it. It's too raw.

BEEZIE

And?

AVA
(inventing)
She's incapacitated. Mom's incapacitated.

Beezie is just looking at her, watching it unfold.

AVA
(got it)
From a stroke! And that's why she hasn't called.

BEEZIE
And is she going to recover?

AVA
Of course not. This is an end-of-life stroke.

BEEZIE
Right. I should've known.

AVA
He'll get the idea. She's not eating—or talking. Can't swallow. Or see, or hear.

BEEZIE
How do we know she can't hear?

AVA
Or move. She just—twitches. And gurgles. She gurgles a lot.

BEEZIE
And when does the gurgling stop?

AVA

When we're on the plane. Outta here.

BEEZIE
(amazed)
You've been planning to lie to him the whole time.

AVA

It's not a lie. It's a precaution.

BEEZIE

About Mom's death? Of course it's a lie. We came out here to tell him, to be with him and help him deal with it.

AVA

Well, it's a white lie then, a beneficial lie—we'll prepare him to deal with it.

BEEZIE

I can't believe you. No, I take that back. I never believe you.

AVA

You don't acknowledge there is such a thing as a beneficial lie— that sometimes lying can be helpful, a necessity?

BEEZIE

How would you know? You lie about everything. You lied about dolls and crayons.

AVA

Wow, this is getting kind of childish.

BEEZIE
(trying to control herself)
You always lie and you always get away with it.

AVA
So—from childhood you couldn't get what you wanted because I lied? And you lost. So your pathetic life is what, my fault?

BEEZIE
(looks at her)
You know what? You are about an inch shy of being as crazy as he is.

AVA
Watch what you say.

BEEZIE
Without his honesty and sweetness. Oh, what'll you do, change my ticket to "economy," take back the wedges, stop "gifting" me?

AVA
You are an ungrateful, self-righteous little twat.

BEEZIE
Right! A little twat who can care for someone other than herself.

AVA
(sarcastic)
You've always been such a caring person.

A pause.

BEEZIE
(revealing a secret, she can't help herself)
Mom left me money to visit Arky.

AVA
(surprised)
Oh. Your own little pay-off. Good for you.

BEEZIE
She figured you might never do it.

AVA
Really? Well fuck her then.

BEEZIE
Because you've been too threatened by what happened to him—
losing his mind, was too close, too You.

AVA
She didn't say that.

BEEZIE
To even go see him. She did!

AVA
No. She wouldn't. That's—really hurtful. And if she did, you are
so—and you're repeating it.

Beezie just looks at her.

AVA
(overcome)

That's cruel! That's so cruel.

In distress, she goes upstage, starts grabbing tubes and jars.

BEEZIE

What are you doing?

AVA
(turns for bedroom)

I'm going home!

BEEZIE

No. Oh no.

AVA

Home!

BEEZIE

We are doing this together.

AVA
(drops a product)

You stay and deal.
(juggles, drops another)
Comfort him. Be the perfect one!

She stomps on the dropped tubes.

BEEZIE

So Mom was right?

AVA

(stops, looks up)

Okay, it scares me! You want points for that? That I'm scared to see him?

BEEZIE

You always treated him like yours—your baby.

AVA

Does it make you feel good hearing it? I'm scared.

BEEZIE

I was so little, and you told me to get my own baby.

AVA

I'm fucking incapable. And this place is a dump!

BEEZIE

I will not do this alone.

AVA

Why not? You're the responsible one, the "together" one, Miss Fucking Girl Scout Cookie.

She's gathering up her products.

BEEZIE

We are going together. He's our responsibility, not mine. Man-up for once, one time, one time and don't run. We are going to tell him, Ava! It could even help us—all three of us. Don't run! Fight it. Fight it off. Don't run. And for fuck's sake don't cry. Mom's dead.

(pauses)

Man up, bitch!

> LIGHTS SHIFT to Arky, two empty coffee cups on the table, working on a third as he looks at newspaper.

ARKY

Running from the bombs
Running for the boats
Everybody running
Running for the White House
Running for the gold
Running from the spouse
Running from the cold
Everybody running
Running for the shore
Running from the mold
Cold scold gold mold
Bombs bombs bombs bombs bombs
Pray for the Muslims
Pray for—

> Beezie and Ava enter Starbucks cautiously, stage left. They look around, spot Arky. Ava reaches for Beezie's hand, grasps it. They hesitate.

Arky looks up, sees them and—a beatific, child-like smile breaks across his troubled face. He rises in delight! They are visibly relieved by his smile. Beezie starts towards him Ava in hand, all grinning.

Arky looks around quickly, looks up. His smile vanishes.

ARKY

Mom's dead!

Beezie and Ava stop in their tracks, dumbfounded.

ARKY

Mom's dead. I just heard Dad's voice. Dad told me, he was crying. I know but how do you cry when you're dead? It's mysterious but I heard Dad crying. And I'm just like him, right? Like Dad? Maybe I am Dad. Mom told me before—she said it's hard, it's hard but it's about who loves you—who you travel with in life. About who loves you. I don't know. Your family, she said. Mom said. She'll talk to me, I know she will. She said . . .
(sings)
"Shine, shine always, shine everywhere, shine like the sun."
(speaks)
That's our motto she said. She sang that to me. I can hear both their voices, and you're here. All of us together, all five of us! Mom's dead. I'll be okay, right? I'm not alone, I'm not alone. I'm never—not alone. I'll be okay! Mom said it's who you travel with in life—it's about who you travel with, she said.

A beat, and Beezie moves towards him, Ava still holding on. He stands still. They are all fearful. A couple feet away Beezie and Ava stop.

Beezie opens her arms towards him. Ava opens her arms. Arky, as if learning how to do it for the first time, opens his arms. No one moves, six open arms.

With a surge of emotion, Ava rushes to embrace her brother, hugs him. Beezie steps forward, hugs the two of them. Arky, slowly, slowly, lowers his arms around his sisters.

LIGHTS gradually fade down, and out.

Scene Three

THE PORT OF MISSING MEN

Ten years later.

LIGHTS come up on a physical therapy space filled with colorful equipment, some actual, some suggested: cycles, free weights, mini-stairs, pulley and weight machines, large rubber balls, stretchy rubber bands, and round squeezable objects.

An open entrance into the area is upstage right. Behind it is an unseen reception/waiting room.

A small desk stacked with clipboards and an open lap-top is down left, angled into the room. On a high shelf down right, a muted TV faces upstage. Upstage center is a narrow therapy table covered with crisp white paper and above it the suggestion of a privacy curtain.

On a counter stage right, steam rises from a small boiler with hot packs. Below it is a mini-freezer with cold packs and a basket stacked with fresh white towels. Two folding chairs are up left, for resting patients.

A closed door stenciled "Massage Room" is upstage left.

One older woman in sweats, MRS. JAX (played by the actor who plays Tess), rides an exercycle as slowly as possible for it to still be in motion.

The other patients are large human-size pillow DUM-MIES—big, puffy pliable people-shaped pillows indivi-dually dressed or with painted-on clothing, as personality might suggest. Two staff members, TONYA, the physical therapist (played by the actor who plays Beezie), and SHELLY, the intern/assistant (played by the actor who plays Ava), are busy with patients as GUS, the trainer (played by the actor who plays Micah), steps out of the massage room carrying a patient, smiling and nodding to the dummy.

The opening moments are a PT ballet—dummy patients are carried station-to-station, huge, floppy and cumber-some, shuffled and manipulated by the fast-moving staff who relate easily to them as they glide the dummies on and off chairs and equipment.

At any given moment, one of the staff will go quickly to the desk, check a clipboard for specific therapy details, grab a cold pack or fresh towel, a cup of water, and quickly return to a patient. The three staff members work together smoothly, battle-tested.

Shelly the intern is continually on the move, taking guid-ance from Gus and Tonya if she is unsure of how to proceed. She's well put together in tight jeans with a short, white hospital jacket. Outgoing and friendly, she supplies ice packs and heat packs, sets timers, gathers equipment, escorts patients to machines, and helps them out of the room.

Gus is genial and buff and at the center of things. He's knowledgeable about each patient's exercise Rx. He instructs, encourages and checks on how they are doing as they work out. It's his roost.

Tonya does most of her PT work with patients on the table, upstage, physically manipulating them and urging them to do the uncomfortable exercises that have been prescribed. All business, she seems to bear a hidden burden.

A timer dings!

MRS. JAX
(stops peddling)

Water.

(raises a hand)

Over here. Water, please. Immediate water!

Shelly has filled a cup, hands it to her.

MRS. JAX
(drinks)

Oh boy. Thank you, dearie.

(points up at the TV)

Imagine that? Such a thing? They let people get into a hospital with an automatic rifle. Well, why not, if that's how you wake up in the morning: I think I'll go shoot some pregnant women and babies?? We live in Crazyland.

SHELLY

More water, Mrs. Jax, another cup?

MRS. JAX

Please just get me the hell off this thing. My kishkas—all this exercise. You know what kishkas are?

Shelly smiles, shakes her head No and helps her off the bike.

MRS. JAX

Just wait.
(*looks her over*)
What you have? All of that—beauty, at some point I'm sorry, it
will loosen up. Turn to kishkas. Don't worry. That fiancé of yours
in Florida? By then?
(*shakes her head*)
He won't notice. He'll be busy emptying his plastic urinal. What's
next? And don't say the pulleys.

SHELLY
(*grins*)
The pulleys.

MRS. JAX

You are a nasty young woman, and blonde.

GUS
(*checks a clipboard*)
Mrs. Jax. Three sets of ten today, each arm ten times. That's thirty
all together, for each arm.

> MRS. JAX
> *(looks at him)*

I can't count?

> GUS
> *(grins)*

I know you can count. I just wasn't sure how high.

> *Shelly stifles a laugh.*

> MRS. JAX

That's funny.

> *(to Shelly)*

You can laugh, dearie, he likes it when you laugh, things jiggle. Ask him if he covered the spread on the Jets yesterday, see if he's still laughing.

> *Gus loses his smile, shakes his head as he goes to another patient.*

> MRS. JAX
> *(points to herself)*

You're looking at a winner! I shouldn't tease him, he's in debt. I can tell by the eyes. And his wife doesn't know. I've been there.

> *She sits at the pulley machine, which Shelly adjusts for her.*

> SHELLY
> *(glances outside)*

God, it's snowing like crazy already, just like they said. Please rest between sets.

MRS. JAX

You think I'm in a hurry?

SHELLY

Just fifteen or twenty seconds.

MRS. JAX

I haven't been in a hurry since nineteen ninety-seven.

A timer dings! Shelly hustles off to another patient as Mrs. Jax begins her very slow pulley workout.

Tonya lowers a patient onto her therapy table.

TONYA
(to dummy patient)

And you've been diligent, doing your exercises at home? A little better? On a scale of ten?
(listens)
Okay, good. Excellent! I've got a new—
(listens)
Oh, thank you, he's—my husband is doing—better. Somewhat. Thank you. Somewhat better. Now I'm going to raise your right leg Arthur, very slowly.

We watch her lift a pillow-leg. Across the room, Gus puts a red rubber stretchy band over his wrists. Demonstrating for a patient as he moves his arms apart.

GUS

Red is the loosest band. We'll gradually move you up to green.
Like this, just as far as you can pull them apart. Try maybe three
or four in a row. Take a breather, do it again.

(calls out)

Shelly, from here Mrs. Kersey goes onto the steps.

*Shelly acknowledges him as she takes a patient towards
the entrance.*

SHELLY

(to patient)

That's a lot of snow expected, eight to twelve inches! Wow. We're
in for it. Are you being picked up?

*She disappears through the opening to the waiting room.
Gus brings a patient to a chair, goes to the desk, checks a
clipboard, takes a sip of water, pulls a cold pack from the
freezer, grabs a clean towel brings them to the dummy patient in the chair and places the pack on a knee.*

GUS

(to patient)

Yes, ice at home too if you can, after you exercise.

*He turns to Tonya at her table, she looks up at him. They
hold a private gaze. He touches her shoulder for longer
than a moment.*

GUS
(upbeat)

So how is Arthur doing?

TONYA

Good, right Arthur?

(listens)

He wants to know when he can run around the block.

GUS

Tonya's the expert, Arthur. Whatever she says.

> *He gives her hand a squeeze as Shelly returns with ARKY. Arky moves slowly, painfully. He looks much older than his years, mid-forties. He wears clean jeans, a fresh shirt, yellow sneakers and a vest.*
>
> *[NOTE: Arky hears voices: his parents' and his sisters'. The voices come from the three PT workers and Mrs. Jax. It happens naturally, fluidly indicated either by a short zither-like thrum, a light shift, an attitudinal shift, or simply by having the actors stop their activities, hold for the family exchange, then continue on as their PT characters. Whatever works best.]*

ARKY
(talking as he enters)

In Poland locked them all in a barn. It was on TV about a book, people talking about a book.

SHELLY
(ignores what he says)
Your social worker said if she can't get back because of the snow
we should call for a taxi. You live at The Port, don't you?

ARKY
(nods)
Locked them up in a barn. Women, children, babies. A small town,
all the Jews, but first they killed the men. Outside the barn. In Poland.

SHELLY
(leads him to the exercycle)
Port Cove Road? She said you know the address—your address.
It's nasty out there.

ARKY
(stops walking)
They burned it. The barn—with the Jews inside. Their neighbors.
In Poland. A small town, not the Nazis. It was—the neighbors.

SHELLY
We'll warm you up on the exercycle. Is that a new vest?

ARKY
Yes. It has a mind of its own. It can blink.

GUS
(calls out)
The Ark-Man arrives!

ARKY
(waves tentatively to Gus)
It was their own neighbors—in Poland. Polish people. Their
neighbors. It's like—I don't know. Terrorists?

GUS
(calls out)
Hey, look at that vest! Pretty fancy, Ark-Man.

*Arky smiles, nods to Gus. Shelly has brought him to the ex-
ercycle.*

ARKY
Then the neighbors stole everything—from their houses. And
they blamed the Nazis. That was their big secret in the village,
even the priests. They knew.

SHELLY
(impatient)
Okay. I'm setting the timer—climb on please.

ARKY
(gets on the exercycle)
It was scary. I watched it—talking about a book. Did you read it,
Shelly?

SHELLY
(moves away)
What? No.

ARKY

On the bike. I can do this.

Arky begins to peddle.

GUS
(to Shelly at the desk, sips water)
Ark-Man going strong.

SHELLY
(checks clipboard)
The stuff he talks about.

ARKY
(to himself, peddling)
Just people. All people, all in the world.

GUS
He's a sweetheart, just ignore the babble. You feeling okay?

SHELLY
Yeah, why?

Gus shakes his head.

SHELLY
What?

GUS
It's just—your jeans are so tight I thought you might be suffo-cat-ing.

She shoots him a look as she grabs a towel, moves to a patient.

GUS

Big snow happening, Ark-Man.

ARKY

(unsure)

I can get back to the house. It's a big storm! Port Cove Road. I'll get back. Number twenty, right?

A thrum comes and goes.

GUS

(as MICAH)

Mom and I have total confidence in you, Arky.

ARKY

(upbeat, peddling)

I can take care of myself, Dad. I can make things happen.

GUS

(as MICAH)

You do. You work hard. Focus on getting better, Arky—on your health. I know you can do that.

ARKY

I will! Dad, I'm afraid—I—maybe I caused the tsunami.

GUS
(as MICAH)

It was an occurrence of nature, Arky . . .

ARKY

But I imagined it! Before it happened.

GUS
(as MICAH)

. . . an act of god. You did not cause the tsunami.

ARKY

But suppose—god was angry at me.

GUS
(as MICAH)

You've done nothing wrong, Arky. God smiles on you every day. Please believe me.

ARKY

I do! Dad—am I you?

GUS
(as MICAH)

You are your own man, dude. You always will be.

ARKY

Okay. So do you think—should I propose? Do you think I should propose?

GUS
(as HIMSELF, picks up a clipboard)
What? Propose what, Ark-Man?

ARKY
(hesitates, low)
To Shelly. Should I propose?

GUS
(considers)
I think it's too soon. She's still an intern.

He moves off to a patient.

ARKY
(peddling)
Okay, thanks Gus, thank you!

Gus waves over his shoulder.

A pause.

MRS. JAX
(on pulleys)
Are we having fun yet?

ARKY
(peddling, concerned)
Are we supposed to?

MRS. JAX

It's a personal decision.

ARKY

Oh. I'm not having fun yet. Are you?

MRS. JAX

I'm having a blast.

ARKY

Really?
(a pause, remembering)
I remember—those songs. That was—the singing. The ukulele!
That was a blast.

SHELLY
(checks his timer)
A few more minutes, then Tonya wants you, Arky.

She moves off.

From their various positions in the room, all four begin to sing as a family, Arky joins in.

GUS, TONYA, SHELLY, MRS. JAX

Yes sir, that's my baby
No sir, I don't mean maybe
Yes sir, that's my baby now . . .
(Arky joins in)
By the way,
Oh by the way,

When we see the preacher we will say
Yes sir . . .

The singing fades out, and they continue their work.

ARKY

All together, the whole family, singing all together. That was a blast.

MRS. JAX
(as TESS, stops exercising)
I asked the girls to call you, sweetheart, call every few days, take turns.

ARKY

They call, Mom. Beezie. Always—mostly Beezie.

MRS. JAX
(as TESS)
And visit. Visit you often, regular visits.

ARKY
(hesitates)
I'm—I don't know. Was it a promise? Or a wish?

MRS. JAX
(as TESS)
They love you, Arky. Your sisters love you always.

ARKY

I know Mom. Ava sends me sneakers. I have a lot of sneakers. Not enough socks.

MRS. JAX
(as HERSELF, exercising, looks at him)
Young man, what you need are boots. Ten inches of snow you don't need sneakers, believe me.

ARKY
(realizes it's not his mother)
I—I hate boots. They remind me of winter.

MRS. JAX

It is winter.

ARKY

Always?

MRS. JAX

What you need are dry feet.

Arky laughs at something internal, peddles. Mrs. Jax shakes her head.

TONYA
(taking dummy Arthur towards the entrance)
Well, my husband can't travel, but I dream about vacations, warm vacations—with coconuts! That's about as close as I can get, a nice long dream. But real travel, around foreigners? I've seen enough on TV. Foreigners are all over the place.

>   *(low)*
> Right next door? Might be a Muslim, maybe two.

> *Hearing the word, Arky looks up as Tonya exits with Arthur.*

>   SHELLY
>   *(taking a patient to a chair)*
> Last storm we lost power for two days. No heat, no TV, no nothing. I'll get you an ice pack.
>   *(About to pass Arky, she stops, holds as AVA)*
> Mom says take a shower—right now.

>   ARKY
>   *(peddling)*
> I already did.

>   SHELLY
>   *(as AVA)*
> Mom says now, with soap.

>   ARKY
>   *(bothered, sharply)*
> I did already!

>   SHELLY
>   *(as HERSELF)*
> Are you talking to me?

ARKY
(frightened)
Hi Shelly! Did I ding yet? I think I dinged.

Annoyed, she checks the timer, shakes her head No, goes for an ice pack

GUS
(at desk)
The ice-queen approaches.

SHELLY
(re Arky)
He's such a nut-job.

GUS
He was an all-star kid—president of his class, basketball captain—then at eighteen or nineteen—boom. His mind just broke. Snapped. Done. Finished.

SHELLY
No! That's awful.

GUS
His social worker told me the whole story. A good family, strong. Sad stuff, sad stuff.
(looks at his clipboard)
We do what we can, we all do what we can.

SHELLY
And what's that supposed to mean.

GUS
(teasing)
Well, I believe Shelly is tied in small knots. And—she needs a cleansing release, a physical release. Shelly's fiancé is far away—far away is the fiancé. And tension is building within. It's—palpable.

SHELLY
(makes a fist)
Oh yeah? You want palpable?

GUS
Find yourself an outlet. It would do you a world of good.

SHELLY
(waves her fist)
Palpable this.

He grins, she moves off, amused, as Tonya reappears. She and Gus look at one another across the room.

MRS. JAX
(to Gus)
So tonight, let me guess—Monday Night Football: you take Detroit and points. Anybody but the Patriots. Am I right?

GUS
(turns away, a laugh)
Mrs. Jax, I would take you and points over the Patriots.

MRS. JAX
(to herself, shaking her head)
Bets with his heart, not his head. That's why he's in debt.

Arky's timer dings! He immediately stops peddling, sits still.

Tonya comes over to him as Gus goes to the desk telephone.

TONYA
Arky, you can get off and follow me.
(she stops, holds, as BEEZIE)
Please stop chewing tobacco, Arky. Please.

ARKY
What? No, Beez, I stopped. I mean I'm trying.

TONYA
(as BEEZIE)
Mom is really upset.

ARKY
I told them. I already promised. I'm stopping.

TONYA
(moving, as HERSELF)
Okay, you did stop, so you should be all warmed up by now.
ARKY
(follows her to table)
What? Oh. I think so. I'm warm!

He climbs onto the table, facing downstage.

GUS
(puts phone down, speaks to the room)
We're going to close early everybody, so we can all get home safe-
ly and in case we lose power. Keep going with your exercises, it
won't be for a little while yet.

MRS. JAX
(on the pulleys)
My arms are about to fall off.

SHELLY
What's next for Mrs. Jax, Gus?

He checks a clipboard.

MRS. JAX
It's like the Inquisition here.

GUS
The steps. At your own pace—five sets of three. That's a total—

MRS. JAX
Stop! Don't insult me.

GUS
(helps her to the steps)
So you took Detroit and the points tonight?

MRS. JAX

Of course. Listen, you shouldn't be gambling. I bet your wife tells you that, too. You're using it as a distraction from something. I don't know what, but I know gamblers.

Surprised, he looks at her as she starts up the steps.

TONYA
(working on Arky's neck and back)

T-O-N-Y-A. Tonya.

ARKY

That's—unique.

TONYA

My father's name is Tony, my mother's name is Ann. So—Tonya.

ARKY

That's a lot of Tony. Not much Ann.

TONYA
(a laugh)

I know. It was his idea.

ARKY
(matter-of-fact)

My father's dead. My mother's dead, too.

TONYA

Oh, I'm so sorry.

ARKY
(shakes his head)
No, it's okay, I can still hear them. And I have two sisters.

TONYA
That's good!

ARKY
(a pause)
I'll keep working hard, Tonya. Then I'll feel better.

TONYA
Absolutely. You sure will.

Mrs. Jax is on the steps, Shelly beside her.

MRS. JAX
Up down, up down. Where's it getting me?

SHELLY
Getting you stronger. Don't your legs feel stronger?

MRS. JAX
Dearie, would it make you happy for me to say Yes?

SHELLY
(smiles)
Well, it's a process—strengthening muscles after long inactivity.

MRS. JAX
"She died with stronger legs."

Gus works with a patient.

GUS

Squeeze these balls, one hand at a time, eight times each, hard as you can. Do three sets of eight.
(grins, nods)
Sure, personalize the balls, pick whoever you want. Squeeze them. The harder you squeeze the better. Go for it.

ARKY
(on the table)
My neck and my back. Once I fell—I—out of a convertible, that was a long time ago. I can't remember the Why of it.

TONYA
(works on him)
Well, the x-rays do show a lot of arthritis.
(stops, holds as BEEZIE)
Arky, Mom's in the kitchen crying.

ARKY

Why? I told her I was stopping.

TONYA
(as BEEZIE)
You haven't stopped the chewing, Arky.

Shelly halts nearby.

> SHELLY
> *(as AVA)*

There's tobacco juice all over the rug, Arky, the living room rug.

> ARKY

I'm trying.

> TONYA
> *(as BEEZIE)*

At least not in the house, Arky.

> SHELLY
> *(as AVA)*

It's a disgusting habit.

> *She moves off.*

> ARKY
> *(feral)*

Leave me alone!

> TONYA
> *(as HERSELF, backs away scared)*

Gus. Gus?

> ARKY
> *(realizing)*

I'm sorry! Sorry Tonya.

> *Gus comes over, Tonya points to Arky on the table. Gus nods.*

GUS
(calm, understanding)

Ark-Man.

He pats Arky's shoulder.

ARKY
(scared)

Sorry, Tonya.

GUS

Take a deep breath, relax. Deep breath. Deeeep breath.

Arky deep-breathes.

GUS
(patting his shoulder)

Okay, we're all working together here.

ARKY

I got—confused.

GUS

Teamwork, right?

ARKY

I know!

GUS

Back on track, Ark-Man?

ARKY

Back. I'm on track. Sorry, Tonya. Back on track.

GUS

Good man.
(reassuringly touches Tonya)
So we'll close early, a little early. We'll have some extra time.

She nods cautiously, goes back to work on Arky.

GUS
(as MICAH)

Mom and I met with him, Arky. It's a suggestion. He's a doctor, he might be helpful.

ARKY
(late teens, on the table)

I don't need any help.

GUS
(as MICAH)

He works with a lot of young people, people your age. Mom liked him, too.

ARKY
(late teens)

So?

GUS
(as MICAH)

I think you'll like him.

He heads off to another patient.

ARKY
(late teens, louder)

Just because you like him?

Gus, as HIMSELF, heads to another patient.

TONYA
(surprised)

Gus? Sure. I mean everybody likes Gus.

The LIGHTS flicker a moment. They all look up. Thunder rumbles.

GUS
(jovial)

Get your flashlights ready!

Shelly is exiting, talking to a patient.

SHELLY

You can't DVR if there's no power, right? So I'll miss all my Monday shows.

Mrs. Jax is finishing at the steps.

ARKY

Tonya, can I tell you a secret?

                    TONYA
                 (apprehensive)
A secret? Are you sure?

                     ARKY
I'm wearing my flashlight—it's on the vest.

                    TONYA
Okay.

                     ARKY
It has a switch. On and off. For Christmas.

                    TONYA
                   (relieved)
Wow. Where did you get that?

                     ARKY
My sister Ava. Not Beezie. Beezie calls.

                    TONYA
That's quite a gift.

                     ARKY
If I remember. To turn it on.

        At the steps, Mrs. Jax grips the bannister.

                     GUS
How are you doing?

MRS. JAX

Who should I ask? I can't tell anymore.

SHELLY

(re-enters)

They've got the plows out already. It's really coming down.

GUS

(guiding Mrs. Jax to a chair near Arky)

Shelly, some water and an ice-pack for Mrs. Jax, please.

MRS. JAX

(as she sits)

One for my neck.

GUS

Make that a double, Shell.

MRS. JAX

So after what just happened in Texas you still think banning assault rifles is a bad idea?

GUS

If a nurse or a doctor had one nearby that maniac would never have made it.

MRS. JAX

(shakes her head)

A doctor with a stethoscope and an AR-15.

GUS
(nods, moving off)
Hey, a lot of lives could've been saved.

MRS. JAX
Maybe we should arm the babies, too.

Shelly comes over with ice packs and water.

MRS. JAX
Small weapons for the babies, say a twenty-two. Then when they get to be about eight or ten, a nice shiny thirty-eight. What do you think about that, dearie?

SHELLY
Guns? I hate guns. I hate the very idea of guns.

MRS. JAX
Good for you.

SHELLY
But we have to be protected, don't we? From whatever?

TONYA
Right at the border, that's where. Keep 'em out.

ARKY
(face down on the table)
Who protects the Muslims? Who protects the Jews?

> TONYA

The Muslims?

> MRS. JAX

Which border?

> TONYA

Whatever. All of them! Okay, Arky, please sit up. Just rest here a few while I check what's next. I think you're on the pulleys, and I have someone in reception.

> ARKY

The what? Oh, the pulleys. Sure, I can do it.

> TONYA

I'll be right back.

> MRS. JAX

She wants to shoot the Canadians, too.

Arky sits up on the table as Tonya moves for the desk.

> MRS. JAX

All this gun talk is making me nauseous.

> ARKY

I throw up when I eat too much chocolate, milk chocolate.

> MRS. JAX

Guns and chocolate, that'll do it.

ARKY

First they shot the men, all the men. Outside the barn.

Tonya moves from desk, exits into reception area. A thrum.

MRS. JAX
(as TESS)

Arky, I'm counting on you to take care of yourself, sweetheart.

ARKY

Okay Mom, but I don't know what to do about the terrorists. Is it my job, Mom? Should I make a plan? I'm—what about the Muslims?

MRS. JAX
(as TESS)

Your job is you. Only you.

ARKY

There's this—this train in my head—loud train roaring—all the time. It's—I try to accomplish things for—for some accomp-lishments, like the girls have. They have accomplishments.

MRS. JAX
(as TESS)

I'm proud of you, Arky. I know it's hard.

ARKY

But it wasn't supposed to be like this! I know it.

MRS. JAX
(as TESS)

You're doing a really good job, sweetheart.

ARKY

A girlfriend, a wife—a whole family—that's what.

MRS. JAX
(as TESS)

I understand.

ARKY

I wish—I wish—

MRS. JAX
(as TESS)

What do you wish?

ARKY

That I could be with you again.

MRS. JAX
(as TESS)

Arky, your sisters love you, too.

ARKY

The girls forget! I miss you so much. They forget to visit.

MRS. JAX
(as TESS)

Love never dies, Arky.

ARKY

Promise? Do you promise?

MRS. JAX
(unsteady, as HERSELF)

Oh boy—

(raises a hand for Shelly)

Dearie?

Shelly is not looking her way. Arky is concerned about Mrs. Jax.

MRS. JAX

I don't feel well at all.

She shakes her head, slumps over.

ARKY
(scared)

Mom? Mrs—are you—Mrs. Jax are you okay?
*(hesitates, looks around for help but no one is looking their way,
      he tries calling out but his voice is tight, strangulated.)*
Gus—

(tries again, fighting panic, same result)

Gus?

(he can't get anyone's attention)

Somebody.

(sound comes out but not loud enough)

Gus!

(he jumps up, lets it rip, bellows!)

GUS!

Gus looks up, sees her, rushes over.

GUS
(on his knees)

Mrs. Jax. Mrs. Jax?

ARKY

Is—is she—

GUS

Mrs. Jax!

ARKY

Is she—

MRS. JAX
(lifts her head)

I'm not deaf.

GUS
(checking her pulse)

Talk to me. How do you feel?

Tonya has returned from reception.

MRS. JAX

Lousy. I took a little snooze.

GUS

You fainted.

                              MRS. JAX
I never faint!

                                ARKY
                            (gaping at her)
You fainted.

                                GUS
Your pulse.
                           (calmly to Arky)
The pulleys, Ark-Man.
                        (points him to the pulleys)
Now please.

                              MRS. JAX
That's a rumor. It's gossip. I never faint.

            Arky makes his way across the room to the pulley machine.
            He sits, watches them. The overhead LIGHTS flicker again.

                                GUS
                      (calls out, points to Mrs. Jax)
Tonya, make the call. Make the call, please.

            Tonya alerted, at the desk, picks up the phone. Arky starts
            working on the pulleys.

                                GUS
Shelly, please bring the wheel chair out.

Shelly hustles into the massage room.

MRS. JAX

I am not going to the hospital.

GUS

What are the odds? I'll take the hospital. You can have no hospital and points.

> *Shelly comes out of the massage room rolling a wheel chair.*

TONYA
(comes over)

Okay, they're close. They were nearby.

> *Gus and Shelly help Mrs. Jax to her feet.*

MRS. JAX

I can get up myself!

> *She can't. They deposit her in the wheelchair.*

GUS
(to the room)

Everybody, we're closing up shop now!
(to Shelly)

Let's be waiting for them. Mrs. Jax, Shelly will stay with you.

> *Shelly starts to wheel her out.*

MRS. JAX

Let me go home—I promise not to sue!

Shelly exits with her. Tonya follows with a patient.

TONYA

(to patient)

There's probably four or five inches out there already. Just drive slowly.

GUS

(taking a patient out)

No, she'll be okay. It's only a precaution, she'll be fine. Not to worry.

We hear an ambulance siren approaching. The overhead LIGHTS flicker and go out.

Only Arky is left in the room. In the dimness, we can still see him using the pulleys.

A long silence.

Two people enter side by side in the dark and move across the space. There's a brief flicker of the LIGHTS, and we see Tonya and Gus kissing passionately at the door to the massage room. He opens the door to let her in. She hesi-tates, unsure.

Angled downstage at the pulleys, Arky does not see Gus and Tonya as they go inside, closing the door behind them.

*The siren stops sounding as the red lights of the ambulance
flash through the windows. Heavy thunder rolls in.*

ARKY
(on the pulleys, worried)

Shelly?

(pause)

How long do I do this?

*The red lights begin to fade as the ambulance pulls away
and the siren sounds again, moving off.*

ARKY

Where is everybody?

(starts to recall a song to calm his anxiety)

Washington—Washington at Valley Forge
Freezing cold but up spoke George
Singing voe doe dee oh
Voe doe dee oh doe

(works the pulleys, remembers another song)

Yes sir, that's my baby
No sir I don't mean maybe
Yes sir, that's my baby now
Bye the way, Oh by the way . . .

A silence. He works the pulleys. Loud thunder.

ARKY

Shelly?

The massage room door opens. Thunder rumbles. Tonya,
distressed, rushes out buttoning and tucking in her shirt. A
beat, and Gus comes hurrying after her. Neither of them
sees Arky as they exit.

ARKY
(working the pulleys)
Shelly, is anybody—are you coming back?

He stops exercising a moment, flips the switch on his vest,
and little bulbs blink on, alternating one after the other.

He continues to work the pulleys, illuminated by his vest.

ARKY
Shine
Wake up and shine
Shine always
Shine everywhere
Wake up and shine
Shine always
Shine everywhere
Shine like the sun
Shine like the sun
Shine like the—
(listens)
Mom?
(realizes)
You know—I don't have to stay here. I don't. There's no rule. I can
go. I can just—go! Any time I want. I can do it. On my own.

(whispers)

Port Cove Road. I know! Thank you. I—no help! No help. I know the way. It's not so far. It's not that far. I'll just—do it. By myself and nobody helps. Just—step up. That's how. On my own. Myself. Do it!

(stops working the pulleys)

Port Cove Road. Port Cove Road. I know.

(as he gets off the pulley machine)

Big snow big snow big snow. I can take good care of myself. You don't worry! Is that—it's who you travel with right? In life. It's who loves you. The whole family! All five of us. Side by side, that's who. Love never dies.

(determined, he turns for the Exit)

I'm all warmed up. So—all warmed up. I know how. Deep, deep, and it's—I can do this! I can. I'm—my own man! Dad? I'm my own man!

The lights on his vest lead Arky towards the exit. All walls drop away—the room disappears.

A roaring white-out slams into Arky. The night explodes around him and he staggers forward braving the storm, one sneaker in front of the other.

LIGHTS begin a slow fade down . . .

Trudging, blizzard-battered, Arky fights for home.

THE END

Acknowledgments

TO THE MEMORY of Richard Gilman, Larry Gelbart, Arnold Weinstein, and John Matthews. They didn't live to read the trilogy, but without the blessing of their lives in my younger life these plays would likely never have been written.

In numerous readings, before small, invited audiences, I worked with wonderful, generous New York actors, primarily the brilliant quartet of Keira Naughton, Clea Alsip, Laila Robbins and my pal Jim Naughton. I'm indebted to them for their astonishing inventiveness and their gracious, unflagging commitment.

For their early response and enthusiasm, I am ever grateful to the late Stanley Kauffmann, and to Robert Brustein and Alec Baldwin. To Tony Roberts, Robert Montgomery (whose exuberance and patience helped to decipher and notate my music for the songs in *Mahalo*), Nancy Montgomery, Paul Bresnick (for his insistence), Susan Duff, Lonnie Carter, Robert Gold, Jay and Barbara Strong, Richard and Joan Liebman-Smith, Barnet Kell-man, Kevin Graham, and Peter Osnos—my constant friendship and gratitude.

David Epstein
July 2023

About the Author

DAVID EPSTEIN'S PLAYS have been produced Off-Broadway, at regional theatres across the country, and abroad. He wrote the screenplay for the film *Palookaville,* which began life at the Sundance Festival, was honored at the Venice Film Festival, and opened in the United States and worldwide to critical acclaim. Mr. Epstein has written screenplays for the major movie studios, and his films have aired frequently on network TV and on PBS.

Mr. Epstein has taught at Colgate University, at NYU, and at Yale. He is a graduate of The Yale School of Drama. He lives with his wife Kate on eastern Long Island and Oahu, Hawaii.

www.ingramcontent.com/pod-product-compliance
Lightning Source LLC
Chambersburg PA
CBHW021608120626
46545CB00001B/123